Strength Fitness

Physiological Principles and Training Techniques

EXPANDED EDITION

Strength Fitness

Physiological Principles and Training Techniques

WAYNE L. WESTCOTT, Ph.D.

ALLYN AND BACON, INC.
Boston   London   Sydney   Toronto

Library of Congress Cataloging in Publication Data

Westcott, Wayne L., 1949–
      Strength fitness.

      Bibliography: p. B1
      1. Muscle strength.   2. Exercise—Physiological aspects.   3. Physical fitness.   4. Physical education and training.   I. Title.
QP321.W44   1982b   613.7′1   81-22826
ISBN 0-205-07747-1   AACR2

Managing Editor: Hiram G. Howard

Printed in the United States of America.

10   9   8   7   6   5   4   3   2   1   87   86   85   84   83   82

For my wife, Claudia

Contents

Preface

As more people begin to appreciate the value of strength fitness, it becomes necessary to carefully examine the physiology of strength development. An understanding of how one's muscles become larger and stronger is basic to designing a successful strength training program. Persons who are knowledgeable regarding the research-based principles and procedures for effective strength training are more likely to achieve their desired training objectives. Furthermore, they generally experience faster rates of strength gain and fewer injuries than exercise enthusiasts who are less well-informed.

The purpose of this book is to present those strength training practices that effectively incorporate the scientific principles of strength development. Research on strength training is discussed in practical terms, and related to specific training procedures. The first part of the book is designed to give the reader a basic understanding of strength physiology and strength training principles. The following sections apply this knowledge to the design of a comprehensive and productive strength training program. Exercises for barbells, dumbbells, Universal Gym, and Nautilus Sports equipment are presented and discussed in terms of muscle function and performance recommendations.

The author believes that strength fitness is important for everyone, because it adds a qualitative aspect to one's lifestyle. It is sincerely hoped that the new strength training concepts presented in this text will help people improve their strength fitness in an efficient and safe manner.

Acknowledgments

The author wishes to acknowledge the invaluable assistance provided by Jake Gonas, Thomas Hamilton, W. C. Hinton, Kathryn Kelley, John Saucier, Ina Spinks, Jackson Stevens, Robert Travis, Claudia Westcott, Warren Westcott, Baldwin's Body Forum, Tallahassee Universal Health Spa, and the Florida State University Football Program. Special appreciation is extended to Richard Baldwin, 1981 Mr. America, and Laura Combs, 1981 Ms. America, for their help in producing this book.

Strength Fitness

Physiological Principles and Training Techniques

Chapter One

What about Weight Training?

It is a common question, asked as frequently by forty-year-olds concerned with improving their physical fitness as by twelve-year-olds interested in making their junior high athletic teams. It is a question being asked more often by girls and women. It is a question that receives varied responses, sometimes arouses emotion, and almost always stimulates interest in the phenomenon of strength development. The question is, "What about weight training?"

This question generally raises a number of other questions. What is muscle strength? How is it developed? Why is it important? How should one train? What about nutrition? What will happen if I start training? What will happen if I stop training? The chapters that follow answer these and other questions related to weight training and strength development.

TRAINING PRINCIPLES AND PRACTICES

In simplest terms, muscles become stronger when they are systematically subjected to progressively heavier workloads. This is a basic principle of strength training, known as the Stress Adaptation Principle. Regardless of the particular exercise equipment or training program utilized, strength will increase when the muscles are forced to work against greater and greater resistance.

Example

One day a young married student was looking stronger than he had looked a few weeks earlier. Upon being asked what he had been doing to increase his strength, he revealed a rather unique training program. He had started doing pushups to develop his upper body muscularity. After achieving a relatively high number of repetitions, he increased the resistance by putting his four-year-old boy on his back while he exercised. His next step was to place his eight-year-old son on his back while he performed the pushups. He continued to add resistance in this manner, and was lifting both his wife and his oldest son at the time of our conversation.

The student was commended for his successful application of the Stress Adaptation Principle, and quickly convinced that a weight training program might be a more effective way to increase muscle strength. I pointed out that bench presses stress the same muscles as pushups, permit smaller increments in resistance, and eliminate the strain of people sitting on your back.

There are several other principles of strength training that should be observed for optimal strength development. These include the principles of Rebuilding Time, Near-Maximum Resistance, Controlled Movement Speed, Full-Range Movements, Muscle Balance, and Training Specificity. It is the incorporation of these fundamental principles, rather than the type of equipment utilized, that produces gains in muscle strength.

In addition to training principles, there are a number of training variables that are directly related to strength development. Exercise selection, exercise sequence, weightloads, repetitions, sets, rest intervals, and training frequency are important considerations in designing a successful strength training program.

Training hard is not nearly as important as training intelligently; and intelligent training requires a basic understanding of those principles and practices that have been shown to positively influence strength development.

REACHING ONE'S STRENGTH POTENTIAL

Contrary to advertisements in popular muscle training magazines, relatively few persons who train with weights ever develop championship physiques. The potential for achieving muscle size and strength is largely determined by one's genetic make-up. However, almost everyone can improve strength fitness through an individualized program of weight training.

The keys to developing larger and stronger muscles are personalized training objectives and personalized training procedures. First, honestly assess your present level of strength fitness. Second, set reasonable goals for the end of your first month of training. Most people who train intelligently experience strength gains of about 4 percent per week. It would therefore be reasonable to expect about a 15 percent increase in exercise weightloads after four weeks of training. Third, learn as much as possible about the principles, procedures, and variables that influence strength development. Fourth, use this knowledge to design a weight training program that is appropriate for your particular situation, and follow it faithfully. Consistency is most important. Without regular and disciplined training, even the best designed program will be unproductive. Fifth, keep accurate records of your individual progress using a daily training log. This information is essential for determining the strengths and weaknesses of the training program, making the appropriate adjustments, and establishing new personal goals.

Persons who train with weights, unlike those who engage in most other athletic activities, have almost complete control over the training variables. They can determine the exact weightloads to be used, the number of sets and repetitions to be performed, the length of the rest intervals, and the training frequency. Strength training is also somewhat unique in that the results are readily apparent to the exerciser and others. Gains in muscle size and strength are usually noticed after three or four weeks of training, and these gains, in turn, provide excellent motivation to continue one's exercise program.

WHY IS STRENGTH IMPORTANT?

Why is it necessary to increase one's muscular strength? After all, most people in the United States have enough strength to meet the demands of their daily routines.

There are actually a number of reasons people engage in strength training programs. For some, it is the challenge of competitive weightlifting or bodybuilding. For others, it is a means to enhance performance in their favorite sport. For still others, it is a way to rehabilitate an injured body part in order to resume normal activity.

Perhaps the most prevalent and least understood reason people train with weights is to add quality to their lives. Many people engage in strength training simply because they look better and feel better when they do. They find the training process enjoyable, and the training product well worth the effort. For most people, controlled physical exertion is a satisfying experience, and increased muscle strength is a gratifying accomplishment. Something about becoming stronger enhances a person's self-image.

Strength training is an excellent activity for people who value physical ability and personal appearance. People who train with weights show a genuine concern for developing their physical potential and for maintaining a strong body. Weight training demonstrates, perhaps better than any other activity, the positive relationship between physical training and physiological improvement. Anyone who is interested in physical fitness should make strength training a regular physical activity.

The chapters that follow present principles and techniques for strengthening the muscles of the body through weight training. (See Figures 1–1a and 1–1b).

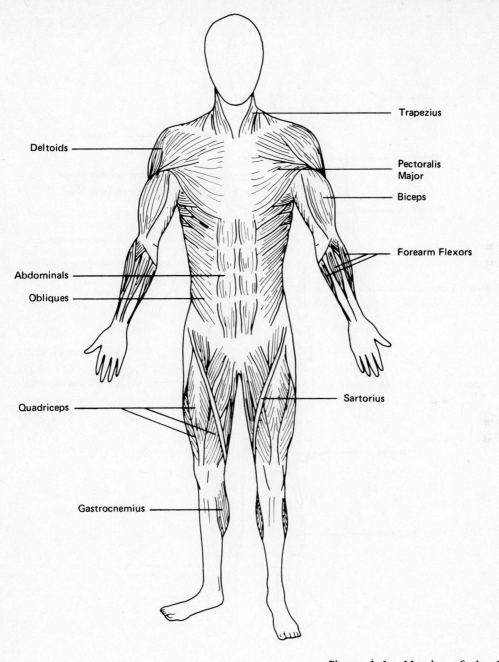

Trapezius

Deltoids

Pectoralis
Major

Biceps

Forearm Flexors

Abdominals

Obliques

Sartorius

Quadriceps

Gastrocnemius

Figure 1–1a Muscles of the Body:
Front

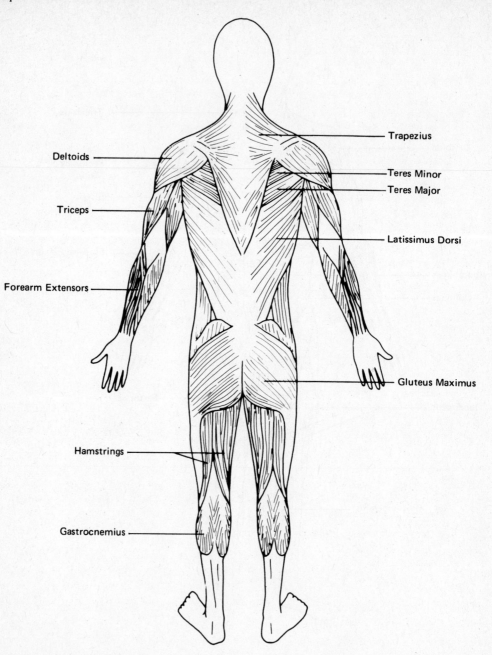

Deltoids

Triceps

Forearm Extensors

Hamstrings

Gastrocnemius

Trapezius

Teres Minor

Teres Major

Latissimus Dorsi

Gluteus Maximus

Figure 1–1b Muscles of the Body:
Back

Chapter Two

Physiology of Strength Development

MUSCLE STRUCTURE

Muscle structure begins with two basic components, thick protein strands, called myosin filaments, and thin protein strands, called actin filaments. Small projections called cross-bridges extend from the myosin filaments to connect them to the surrounding actin filaments. Figure 2–1 illustrates schematically the way these filaments are arranged in a functional contractile unit known as a *sarcomere*.

Adjacent sarcomeres form myofibrils, which are the principle threads running throughout the muscles. Groups of myofibrils are bound together by a membrane called sarcolemma to form individual muscle fibers. Muscle fibers, in turn, are bound together by a membrane called perimysium into bundles of fibers known as fasiculi. These bundles of fibers are enclosed by a connective tissue called epimysium and function together as a muscle, such as the biceps. The structural and functional components of skeletal muscle are shown in Figure 2–2.

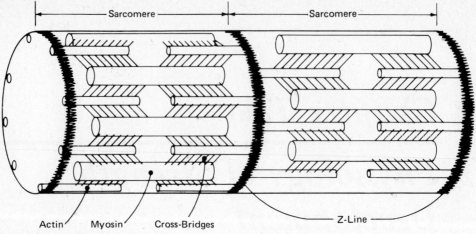

Figure 2–1 The smallest functional unit of muscle contraction, the sarcomere, consists of thin actin filaments, thick myosin filaments, and tiny cross-bridges which serve as coupling agents between the myosin proteins and the surrounding actin proteins.

MUSCLE PHYSIOLOGY

The most important components of skeletal muscle are the contractile proteins, actin and myosin. When activated, the thin actin filaments are pulled toward the center of the thick myosin filaments by the cross-bridges, which enables cross-linkages between the actin proteins and myosin proteins to occur.

The energy necessary for muscular movement is obtained from a rapid series of events beginning with nervous stimulation of the muscle cell. Upon receiving the nerve impulse, calcium ions are released from the sarcoplasmic reticulum, a system of tubules that has storage and distribution functions, and inactivate an inhibitory protein called troponin. When troponin is inactivated, myosin proteins function enzymatically to split adenosine triphosphate (ATP) into adenosine diphosphate (ADP) and energy. This ATP-splitting activity appears to take place at the cross-bridges, providing the energy for the actin-myosin cross-linkages which are responsible for muscular movement.

Upon cessation of nervous stimulation, the calcium ions are re-

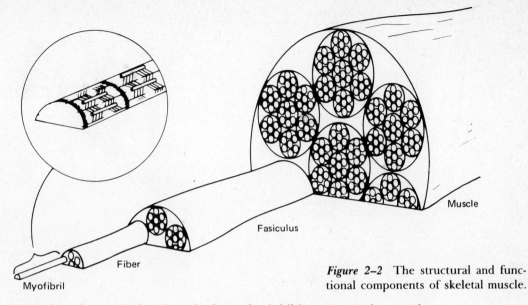

Myofibril   Fiber   Fasiculus   Muscle

Figure 2–2 The structural and functional components of skeletal muscle.

bound to the sarcoplasmic reticulum, the inhibitory troponin proteins are reactivated, the enzymatic activity of the myosin proteins is prohibited, the ATP molecules are not split, energy is not released, crosslinkages do not occur, and the muscle relaxes.

MUSCLE FUNCTION

The function of skeletal muscle is to produce tension (force) which is generally translated into movement. Muscles are attached to bones by connective tissue called tendons. Tendons are actually extensions of the perimysium and epimysium, which enclose the muscle fibers and fiber bundles respectively. As illustrated in Figure 2–3, a skeletal muscle is attached between two bones. Contraction of the muscle produces force, which can move one bone through a range of degrees toward the other bone. The bone that remains stationary is considered the origin of the muscle and the bone that moves is referred to as the insertion.

Joint Movements

The focus of this book is movement about the major joints of the human body. More specifically, exercises that, when properly applied,

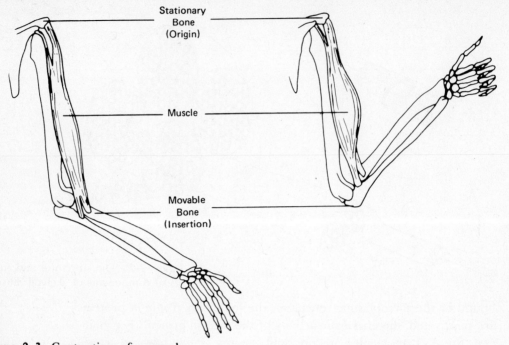

Stationary
Bone
(Origin)

Muscle

Movable
Bone
(Insertion)

Figure 2–3 Contraction of a muscle
resulting in the movement of one bone
toward another. The stationary bone
is referred to as the muscle origin, and
the movable bone as the muscle insertion.

can increase the muscular force of the following joint movements will
be presented. The joint movements are illustrated schematically in Figure 2–4.

Elbow Flexion: Decreasing the angle between the lower arm and
the upper arm.

Elbow Extension: Increasing the angle between the lower arm and
the upper arm.

Knee Flexion: Decreasing the angle between the lower leg and the
upper leg.

Knee Extension: Increasing the angle between the lower leg and the
upper leg.

Shoulder Adduction: Decreasing the angle between the upper arm
and the side (downward-sideward movement).

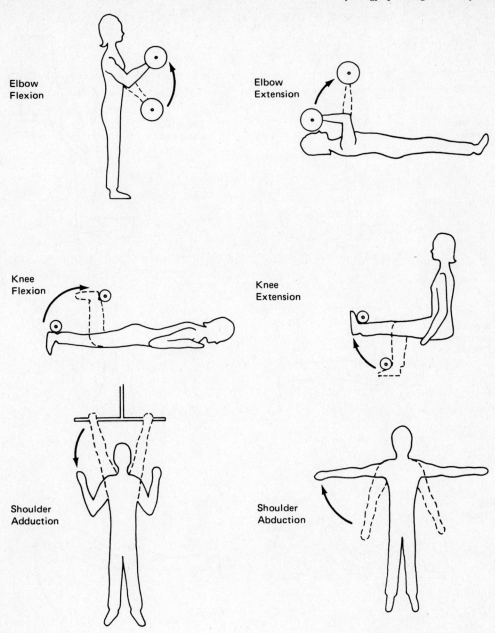

Elbow Flexion

Elbow Extension

Knee Flexion

Knee Extension

Shoulder Adduction

Shoulder Abduction

Figure 2–4 Schematic illustrations of joint movements.

Shoulder
Flexion

Shoulder
Extension

Shoulder
Horizontal
Flexion

Shoulder
Horizontal
Extension

Hip
Flexion

Hip
Extension

Figure 2–4   (*continued*)

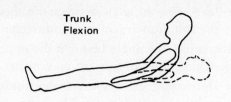

Trunk
Flexion

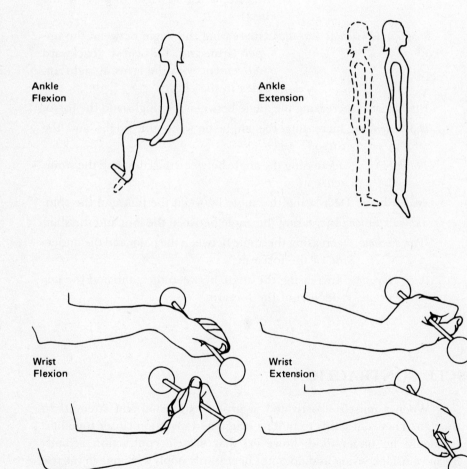

Ankle
Flexion

Ankle
Extension

Wrist
Flexion

Wrist
Extension

Figure 2–4 *(continued)*

Shoulder Abduction: Increasing the angle between the upper arm and the side (upward-sideward movement).

Shoulder Flexion: Increasing the angle between the upper arm and the chest (upward-forward movement).

Shoulder Extension: Decreasing the angle between the upper arm and the chest (downward-backward movement).

Shoulder Horizontal Flexion: Decreasing the angle between the upper arm and the chest (forward movement with the arms at right angles to the chest).

Shoulder Horizontal Extension: Increasing the angle between the upper arm and the chest (backward movement with the arms at right angles to the chest).

Hip Flexion: Decreasing the angle between the thighs and the torso.

Hip Extension: Increasing the angle between the thighs and the torso.

Trunk Flexion: Decreasing the angle between the chest and the stomach.

Ankle Flexion: Decreasing the angle between the foot and the shin.

Ankle Extension: Increasing the angle between the foot and the shin.

Wrist Flexion: Decreasing the angle between the palm and the underside of the forearm.

Wrist Extension: Increasing the angle between the palm and the underside of the forearm.

GROSS MUSCLE CONTRACTION

When a muscle is activated, it produces tension and attempts to shorten. That is, it tends to pull its origin and insertion closer together. It should be understood, however, that muscle contraction actually means muscle tension and does not necessarily imply a change in muscle length. A contracting muscle may actually shorten, lengthen, or remain the same size.

Concentric Contraction

When a barbell is pressed from one's chest during the bench press exercise, the chest and triceps muscles exert force, shorten, and overcome the weightload. Whenever a muscle exerts force, shortens, and overcomes a resistance, it is said to contract concentrically. Concentric contractions are essential for overcoming the force of gravity and for enabling the exerciser to perform lifting movements.

Eccentric Contraction

When a barbell is lowered to one's chest during the bench press exercise, the chest and triceps muscles exert force, lengthen, and are overcome by the weightload. Whenever a muscle exerts force, lengthens, and is overcome by a resistance it is said to contract eccentrically. It should be noted that if the chest and triceps muscles did not exert force during the lowering phase of the bench press exercise the bar would drop onto the chest with the full force of gravity and cause considerable harm to the lifter. Eccentric contractions are, therefore, important for attenuating the force of gravity and for enabling the exerciser to perform safe, controlled lowering movements.

Isometric Contraction

If a barbell is momentarily held six inches above the chest during the bench press exercise, the chest and triceps muscles exert force, but do not change in length. They neither overcome the weightload nor are they overcome by the weightload. When a muscle exerts force, but does not change in length, it is said to contract isometrically. In other words, the force exerted by the muscle is equal to the force exerted by the resistance and no movement occurs. Isometric contractions are important for stabilizing movements and for maintaining given joint positions.

Prime Mover Muscles

In any given joint action, the muscle that contracts concentrically to accomplish the movement is termed the prime mover. The prime mover, then, is the muscle that is principally responsible for the movement. For example, the biceps muscles are principally responsible for elbow flexion, and are, therefore, the prime mover muscle group for elbow flexion exercises, such as barbell curls. (See Chapter Six.) Many exercise movements involve more than one prime mover muscle group. Pull-ups, for example, require both shoulder extension and elbow flexion. (See Chapter Six.) In this case, both the latissimus muscles, principally responsible for shoulder extension, and the biceps muscles, principally responsible for elbow flexion, are prime mover groups.

Antagonistic Muscles

The muscle that produces the opposite joint action to that of the prime mover is called the antagonist. Because it extends the elbow, the triceps muscle is the antagonist to the biceps muscle. On the other hand, the triceps are prime mover muscles for elbow extension exercises, such as triceps press-downs. (See Chapter Six.) For smooth elbow flexion, the triceps (antagonist muscles) must relax and lengthen as the biceps (prime mover muscles) contract and shorten. Conversely, for smooth elbow extension, the biceps (antagonist muscles) must relax and lengthen as the triceps (prime mover muscles) contract and shorten.

Stabilizer Muscles

For the desired movements to occur in certain joints, other joints must be stabilized. For example, to perform a standing barbell curl, the hips, back, and shoulders must be held in a stable position. Otherwise, instead of the barbell being curled to the shoulder, the shoulder girdle might be bent forward to the barbell. A similar situation occurs when performing pushups. The midsection muscles must contract isometrically to maintain the body in a rigid position, thereby enabling one to exercise the chest and triceps muscles through a greater range of motion on each repetition. Muscles that perform this joint stabilizing function act as stabilizer muscles.

CELLULAR MUSCLE CONTRACTION

Muscle contraction is the development of tension (force) within the muscle. Through a series of complex electrical and chemical changes, energy (ATP) is released, cross-linkages occur between the actin and myosin filaments, and both ends of the sarcomere are pulled toward the center. In the case of a concentric contraction, the muscle shortens, overcomes the external resistance, and accomplishes positive work. As the adjacent sarcomeres contract synchronously, the ends of the muscle move toward each other and produce the characteristic bulge schematically illustrated in Figure 2–5.

Motor Unit

Muscle contraction is regulated by the motor unit. A motor unit is made up of a single motor neuron and all the muscle fibers that receive stimulation from that nerve. (See Figure 2–6). In large muscles, such as the rectus femoris, a single motor neuron may innervate several hundred muscle fibers. In smaller muscles that produce precise movements, such as the muscles that move the eyes, each motor neuron

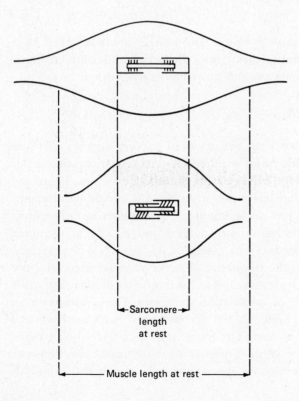

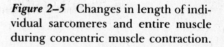

Figure 2–5 Changes in length of individual sarcomeres and entire muscle during concentric muscle contraction.

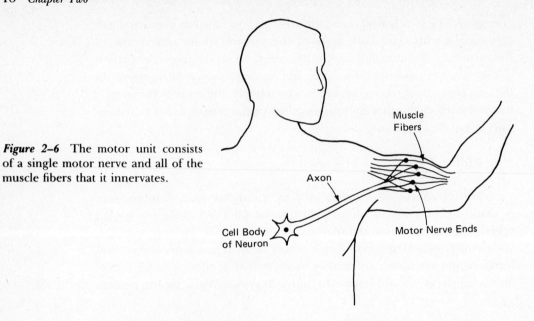

Figure 2–6 The motor unit consists of a single motor nerve and all of the muscle fibers that it innervates.

innervates only a few muscle fibers. The muscle fibers supplied by a motor neuron are distributed throughout the muscle and contract almost simultaneously to facilitate smooth muscular movements.

Force Regulation

Because muscles are required to exert varying degrees of force (e.g., placing a light bulb in an overhead socket versus pressing a 90-pound barbell), some type of regulatory system is essential. There are actually three factors that affect the strength of a muscle contraction. These are the frequency of nerve impulses, the number of motor units activated, and the synchronization of nerve impulses. Fine adjustments in muscle tension are produced by *changes in the frequency of nerve impulses* to the muscle fibers. As the frequency of nerve impulses increases, the strength of contraction increases, and as the frequency of nerve impulses decreases, the strength of contraction decreases. Gross variations in muscle tension are dependent upon the *number of motor units activated* by the central nervous system. The more units recruited, the stronger the contraction and vice versa. Under normal circumstances, different motor units fire independently. When maximum strength is required, however, nervous *impulses arrive synchronously* so that the muscle fibers contract in unison and produce maximum tension.

Fiber Types

Although the strength of contraction in skeletal muscles is primarily regulated by the central nervous system, the individual muscle fibers possess different contractile capacities. Individual muscle fibers may have fast-twitch characteristics or slow-twitch characteristics. Fast-twitch muscle fibers have a greater capacity for anaerobic energy production, and are recruited for activities that require maximum force for short periods of time. Slow-twitch muscle fibers have a greater capacity for aerobic energy production, and are recruited for activities that require submaximum force for long periods of time. For example, a 20-mile bicycle ride would make greater use of the quadricep's slow-twitch fibers, whereas a set of heavy squats would make greater use of the quadricep's fast-twitch fibers.

Fast-twitch motor units have more muscle fibers, larger muscle fibers, and larger motor neurons than slow-twitch motor units, making them better suited for strength production. Although heredity is responsible for one's muscle fiber make-up, training is the most important factor in developing muscular strength. Figure 2–7 illustrates that, as a group, successful weightlifters have about the same percentage of fast-twitch muscle fibers as untrained individuals. It is interesting to note that, as a group, top-ranked distance runners have a much higher percentage of slow-twitch muscle fibers than non-athletes and weightlifters.

Fiber Arrangement

Another factor that influences the strength of contraction is the muscle fiber arrangement. There are basically two types of fiber patterns, fusiform and penniform. Fusiform muscles have long fibers that run parallel to the line of pull. Muscles of this type produce little force, but have a large range of movement. The biceps femoris muscle of the hamstrings group is fusiform. Penniform muscles have short fibers that run diagonally to the line of pull. Penniform muscles, therefore, produce greater force, but have a smaller range of movement. Figure 2–8 presents schematic drawings of a fusiform muscle and two types of penniform muscles, penniform unipennate and the stronger penni-

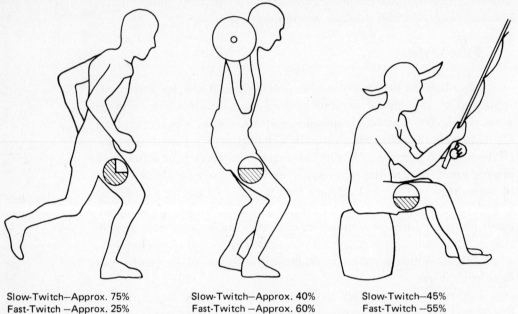

Slow-Twitch—Approx. 75%   Slow-Twitch—Approx. 40%   Slow-Twitch—45%
Fast-Twitch —Approx. 25%   Fast-Twitch —Approx. 60%   Fast-Twitch —55%

Figure 2–7   Distribution of muscle fiber types in distance runners, weightlifters, and untrained males.

form bipennate. The semitendinosus muscle of the hamstrings group is penniform unipennate, and the rectus femoris muscle of the quadriceps is penniform bipennate.

Muscle Relaxation

The natural state of skeletal muscle is called relaxation. It is recalled that skeletal muscle contracts only upon nervous stimulation to do so. In the absence of such stimulation, the contractile mechanism is inactive and muscular tension is not developed. Nonetheless, in a conditioned muscle, a firmness persists even when the muscle is relaxed. This is apparently due to the inherent characteristics of conditioned muscle fibers and connective tissue, and is generally referred to as muscle tone.

Another important aspect of muscle relaxation is the ability of an antagonistic muscle to relax when a prime mover muscle contracts. This process is known as reciprocal innervation, and it is essential for coordinated movements. At the same time that the prime mover muscle is

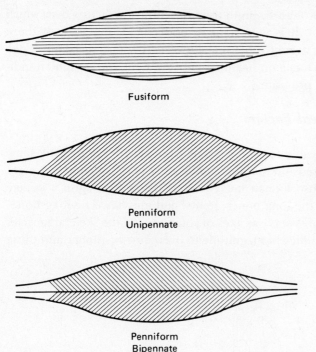

Fusiform

Penniform
Unipennate

Penniform
Bipennate

Figure 2–8 Schematic representations of a fusiform muscle, a unipennate muscle, and a bipennate muscle.

cued to contract and shorten, the antagonist muscle is cued to relax and lengthen. Actually, the degree of tension in each of the opposing muscle groups (prime movers and antagonists) is precisely regulated by the nervous system to enable smooth movements with varying degrees of speed and force.

Muscle relaxation is essential to joint flexibility. Just as a muscle must be trained to contract more forcefully, it must also be trained to relax more completely. When a muscle is stretched to the point of resistance, then maintained in that position for several seconds, it will adjust to its new length, relax, and allow itself to be stretched further.

FACTORS THAT AFFECT STRENGTH

There are several factors besides the physiological properties of the muscle tissue that influence one's effective muscular strength. These include biomechanical factors, lever arrangements, size factors, sex factors, and age factors. With the exception of cross-sectional size, which can be increased through strength training, these are factors over which we have no control. It is important to understand how each of these factors affects one's strength potential, however, because such knowledge helps the exerciser focus on personal improvement and design an individualized training program.

Biomechanical Factors

It is quite possible for two persons who have developed the same amount of muscle tension to differ significantly in the amount of weight they can lift, because human movement is dependent upon a system of levers involving the long bones, joints, and muscles. The long bones act as levers, the joints serve as axes of rotation, and the skeletal muscles produce forces of sufficient magnitude to overcome resistance and cause movement.

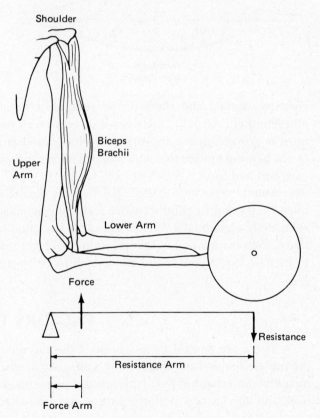

Figure 2-9 The biceps muscle operates as a third-class lever during elbow flexion. The movement force is between the axis of rotation and the resistance.

Figure 2–9 illustrates a lever arrangement that is common in the human body. The biceps muscle operates as a third-class lever with respect to elbow flexion because the movement force is between the axis of rotation and the resistance. The distance between the axis of rotation (elbow) and the force (biceps insertion) is called the force arm, and the distance between the axis of rotation and the resistance (dumbbell) is called the resistance arm. The product of the resistance times the resistance arm is equal to the product of the force times the force arm. Therefore, to determine how heavy a dumbbell one can hold at 90 degrees elbow flexion one must multiply the muscular force by the force arm and divide the product by the resistance arm.

Example

John has a 12-inch forearm with a biceps insertion 1½ inches from the elbow joint. If John can produce 200 pounds of force in his biceps muscle, how heavy a dumbbell can he hold at 90 degrees elbow flexion? (Disregard the weight of his forearm).

$$\text{Muscle Force} \times \text{Force Arm} = \text{Resistance} \times \text{Resistance Arm}$$

$$\frac{\text{Muscle Force} \times \text{Force Arm}}{\text{Resistance Arm}} = \text{Resistance}$$

$$\frac{200 \text{ pounds} \times 1.5 \text{ inches}}{12 \text{ inches}} = 25 \text{ pounds}$$

John's maximum biceps contraction of 200 pounds of muscle tension could hold a 25 pound dumbbell at 90 degrees elbow flexion.

This hypothetical example demonstrates that levers upon which force is applied close to the axis of rotation require relatively large amounts of muscle force to overcome relatively small amounts of resistive force. Although this creates a mechanical disadvantage in movement force, it enables high rates of movement speed, which are vital to most athletic activities.

Although progressive and systematic strength training is the key to developing muscle strength and hypertrophy, it should be understood that certain biomechanical factors affect one's ability to lift heavy weights.

Consequently, one should not become discouraged if one trains as hard as a friend, but cannot perform as well with heavier weights. The friend may simply have a built-in mechanical advantage.

Example

Bob also has a 12-inch forearm but his biceps insertion is 2 inches from the elbow joint. If Bob can produce 200 pounds of force in his biceps muscle, how heavy a dumbbell can he hold at 90 degrees elbow flexion? (Disregard the weight of the forearm.)

$$\text{Muscle Force} \times \text{Force Arm} = \text{Resistance} \times \text{Resistance Arm}$$

$$\frac{\text{Muscle Force} \times \text{Force Arm}}{\text{Resistance Arm}} = \text{Resistance}$$

$$\frac{200 \text{ pounds} \times 2 \text{ inches}}{12 \text{ inches}} = 33.3 \text{ pounds}$$

Bob's maximum biceps tension of 200 pounds is equal to John's. However, due to a biceps insertion that is more favorable with respect to movement force, Bob can hold 33 percent more weight (33.3 pounds versus 25 pounds) at 90 degrees elbow flexion.

This example illustrates that certain inherited factors can profoundly influence one's effective muscular strength. It is therefore important to avoid comparisons with other persons when evaluating a training program. It is essential to realize personal improvement and to strive for individual goals, regardless of the progress, or lack of progress, that others experience.

Third-Class Levers. Levers are classified according to the location of the axis of rotation, the resistive force, and the movement force. In a lever of the third class, the movement force is applied between the axis of rotation and the resistance as shown in Figure 2–10. Because the biceps muscle inserts between the elbow joint (axis of rotation) and the hand (place where resistance is applied), it acts as a third-class lever. Most of the skeletal muscles function as third-class levers. As previously indicated, third-class levers favor movement speed over movement force.

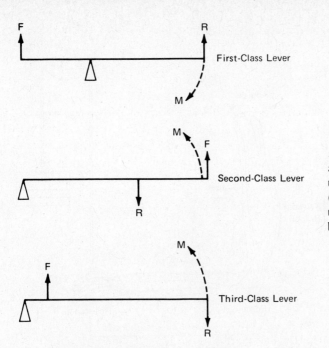

First-Class Lever

Second-Class Lever

Third-Class Lever

Figure 2–10 Three classes of levers as determined by the arrangement of the movement force (F), the resistance (R), and the axis of rotation. The resultant rotational movement is indicated by a broken line (M).

Second-Class Levers. Levers of the second class place the resistance between the axis of rotation and the movement force. (See Figure 2–10.) This arrangement provides great movement force, but is uncommon in the human body. One of the few examples of the operation of a second-class lever is opening one's mouth when chewing taffy or some other substance that resists pulling the teeth apart.

First-Class Levers. In first-class levers the axis of rotation is between the movement force and the resistance, causing the ends of the lever to move in opposite directions. (See Figure 2–10.) The first-class lever arrangements found in the human body are similar to the third-class lever arrangements in that they provide excellent movement speed at the expense of movement force. The triceps muscle is an example of a first-class lever because the elbow joint (axis of rotation) is between the muscle insertion and the hand (place where resistance is applied) as illustrated in Figure 2–11.

Size Factors

While it is true that biomechanical factors have an influence on one's ability to lift heavy weights, the contractile strength of a muscle is most

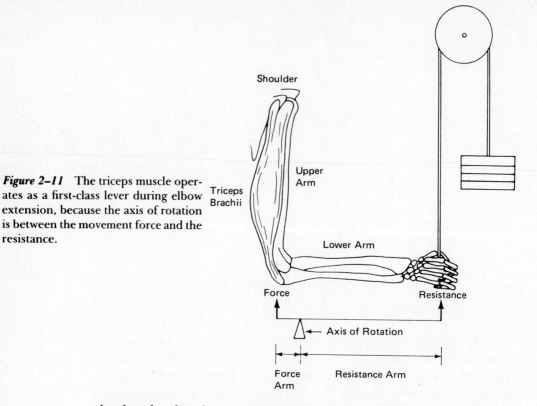

Figure 2–11 The triceps muscle operates as a first-class lever during elbow extension, because the axis of rotation is between the movement force and the resistance.

closely related to its cross-sectional size. For example, triceps muscle can produce approximately 2.88 pounds of force per square centimeter of cross-sectional area. It stands to reason, therefore, that the larger the cross-sectional area the greater total force the triceps muscle can exert.

The cross-sectional area of one's muscles is initially determined by heredity, and a large-framed individual is likely to have larger muscles than a small-framed person. However, strength training can increase the cross-sectional size of a muscle by adding contractile proteins, actin and myosin. Although there is some evidence that strength training can increase the total number of muscle fibers through the process of fiber splitting, physiologists agree that greater muscle size results from the enlargement, not proliferation, of individual muscle fibers. This increase in the cross-sectional size of a muscle as a result of strength training is called *hypertrophy*. Conversely, the decrease in muscle size that occurs when training is discontinued is known as *atrophy*.

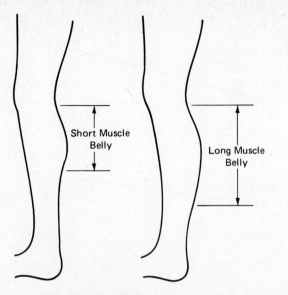

Figure 2–12 Comparison of a short-belly and long-belly gastrocnemius muscle. The length of the muscle belly may affect the potential size and strength of a muscle.

The length of the muscle belly may also be an important factor with respect to muscle size. (See Figure 2–12.) The muscle belly represents the actual muscle length between the tendon attachments. Other things being equal, it is assumed that the person with a longer muscle belly has the potential to develop greater muscle size and strength than the person with a shorter muscle belly. The length of the muscle belly appears to be an inherited characteristic which cannot be changed through training.

Sex Factors

Women who engage in strength training programs develop muscular strength at about the same rate as men. Research by Westcott (1974, 1976, 1979*a*) indicates that both males and females can increase the strength of their bench press muscles (chest, anterior shoulders, and triceps) by between 2 and 6 percent per week depending on age factors and the training program utilized. It also is known that males and females do not differ in strength per square centimeter of cross-sectional area of muscle. However, with respect to muscle size and effective muscle strength there are definite sex-related differences. Although males and females gain strength at similar rates, post-pubescent males begin with larger muscles, which provides a significant strength advantage. Furthermore, strength training increases muscle size to a far greater degree

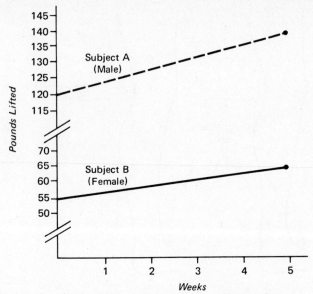

Figure 2–13 Increase in bench press strength as indicated by actual amount of weight lifted. (Bodyweights: male = 160 lbs, female = 95 lbs.)

in males than in females. The reason appears to be related to the male sex hormone, testosterone, which plays a major role in muscle growth and hypertrophy.

By virtue of their genetic make-up, males have a greater potential for muscle size and strength than females. Nonetheless, most females can develop pound-for-pound muscle strength that compares favorably to that of their male counterparts. Figures 2–13 and 2–14 illustrate the strength development of a typical college-age male and college-age female over a five-week training period utilizing the bench press exercise. As shown in Figure 2–13, the male subject increased his bench press by 20 pounds during the training period and the female subject increased her bench press by 10 pounds. When examined in terms of percentage improvement, however, both subjects gained strength at about the same rate, approximately 3½ percent per week. (See Figure 2–14.) It appears that females may obtain the same strength benefits as males from participation in similar strength training programs.

Age Factors

Males and females gain strength through the process of maturation. However, unless they engage in strength training activities, their strength

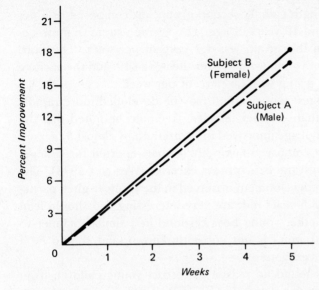

Figure 2–14 Increase in bench press strength as indicated by percent improvement. (Bodyweights: male = 160 lbs, female = 95 lbs.)

begins to decrease at about age 25. This phenomenon is not irreversible, as evidenced by the large number of older weightlifting record holders and physique champions. The key to strength improvement at any age is systematic and progressive strength training. However, research by Westcott (1979*a*) indicates that the rate of strength development may be related to age, at least in females. (See Table 2–1.) Westcott compared the average weekly strength gains for three groups of female subjects training with the bench press exercise. One group consisted of young girls under 13.5 years of age. On the average, the girls in this group increased their strength by 6.4 percent per week, which is an exception-

Table 2–1 Rates of Strength Development for Female Subjects of Different Ages

Age Group	Average Strength Increase Percent per Week
9–13.5 years	6.4
13.5–19 years	4.7
19–27 years	2.6

ally high rate of strength gain. A second group was composed of older girls between 13.5 and 19 years of age. The average strength improvement for the girls in this group was 4.7 percent per week. The third group was made up of young women over the age of 19, and the average strength gain in this group was 2.6 percent per week.

These data suggest that strength may be developed more rapidly in younger females than in older females. It should be noted that the women over 19 years of age improved their strength by almost 3 percent per week, a rate that compared favorably to that reported for college-age males training with the bench press exercise (Westcott 1974). The high rates of strength development observed in the younger girls, particularly those under 13.5 years old, are very interesting and should lead to further study. Whether young boys respond in a similar manner to systematic strength training is not currently known, and should be a subject for further investigation.

The author has found no reason to restrict young children from strength training activities. Clarke's (1971) longitudinal study of boys in Medford, Oregon, revealed a consistent ratio of strength to size during ten years of growth (ages 8–18). Empirical evidence suggests that young children are generally more capable of handling their bodyweight (e.g., climbing trees, ropes, flagpoles) than are adolescents or adults. For those children who are not strong enough to lift their bodyweight, it is far more beneficial to curl a barbell ten times than to struggle with a single pull-up. Both the physical strain and the mental trauma that accompany unsuccessful attempts at bodyweight exercises are unnecessary and can be avoided through weight training activities. Perhaps the greatest advantage of weight training over bodyweight exercises is that the resistance can be accommodated to the strength of each individual, regardless of size, sex, or age.

Training Specificity

People frequently equate hard work with success, but this is only true when there is a strong relationship between the work being done and the desired outcomes. Both a ten-mile run and three sets of heavy squats are hard work, but the physiological responses to each type of exercise are quite different. Both the serious distance runner and the serious weightlifter train an hour or more each day, but their physical appearances are strikingly dissimilar. Training that involves long periods of low intensity exercise develops endurance, but does not improve muscle strength. Conversely, training that involves short periods of high intensity exercise develops muscle strength, but does not improve endurance. Experiments with laboratory animals (Gordon 1967) indicate that endurance training produces an increase in endurance enzymes, but a decrease in contractile proteins, and that strength training produces an increase in contractile proteins, but a decrease in endurance enzymes.

One must train in a specific manner to obtain specific results; strength training for strength development, endurance training for endurance development. Figure 2–15 indicates the approximate positions of various activities along the strength-endurance continuum. Note that strength-related activities are of relatively high intensity and short duration, whereas endurance-related activities are of relatively low intensity and long duration.

Alarm

One occasionally reads of an incredible feat of strength, such as a mother lifting a car off a child pinned beneath it. Such incidents suggest that each of us possesses greater strength than we ordinarily use or even realize we have. Apparently, certain mechanisms within the neuromuscular system prevent the muscles from producing the maximum force possible except under conditions of alarm, thereby protecting the mus-

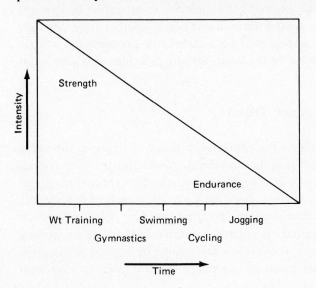

Figure 2–15 Position of various activities along the strength-endurance continuum. Note that strength-related activities are of relatively high intensity and short duration.

cles and connective tissues from possible injury. Strength coaches who are aware of this phenomenon sometimes shout at an athlete during a lifting attempt in order to reduce these built-in inhibitions and trigger more powerful muscle contractions. Perhaps more important, Ikai and Steinhaus (1961) have indicated that one of the effects of progressive strength training is a resetting of the neuromuscular inhibition level, which permits the athletes to voluntarily use a greater percentage of their maximum strength. In other words, well-trained individuals are capable of using some of their reserve strength under normal training conditions.

Muscle Stretch

One of the factors that influences the strength of a muscle contraction is the initial length of the muscle fibers. A muscle produces greater tension when it is stretched just prior to contraction. Ask a friend to perform a standing long jump. Notice that the thigh muscles are momentarily placed on stretch by a quick sitting movement just before they contract powerfully and propel the body several feet through space. Similar pre-stretching movements can be observed in the leg, torso, and shoulder muscles of shot putters as they impart force to the 16-pound ball. Likewise, when one stretches the chest muscles immediately before beginning the upward phase of the bench press exercise considerably more force can be exerted. Although the mechanisms that enable a muscle to generate greater force upon being stretched are not fully understood, it would appear that both the elastic properties of muscle tissue and the alignment of the actin and myosin filaments are major contributing factors.

Variable Resistance Training

As a muscle moves a joint through a range of degrees, the angle of muscle pull changes and the movement mechanics are correspondingly altered. In other words, the effective muscle force varies throughout the range of joint movement, because each joint angle has a slightly different mechanical advantage or disadvantage. The position in which the mechanical disadvantage is greatest is often referred to as the sticking point of the movement. More muscle force must be applied at this position than at any other point in the range of movement to overcome the external resistance. If a barbell can be lifted through the sticking point the entire movement can usually be completed, because less muscle force is required in all other joint positions.

Barbell training has been criticized for requiring maximum muscle exertion at only one position, namely the sticking point of the movement. For this reason, some strength coaches insist that variable resistance training is superior to conventional barbell training. Variable resistance training uses machines that automatically change the resistance and place near-maximum stress on the muscles through the entire range of movement. This can be accomplished by means of moving fulcrums (e.g., Universal Gym), oval-shaped cams (e.g., Nautilus Sports), and hydraulic speed governors (e.g., Mini-Gym). Training on these devices theoretically enables the exerciser to apply maximum muscle tension during every phase of the movement. Because this type of training is extremely demanding on the muscles, persons who work out on variable resistance machines are usually instructed to perform only one set to the point of complete muscle fatigue with each exercise. The weightload is generally adjusted so that muscle failure occurs between 8 and 12 repetitions. For comparison, persons who train with free weights usually execute 3 to 5 sets of 8 to 12 repetitions with near-maximum resistance.

People have many reasons for engaging in strength training programs, but few will persist unless they find the process enjoyable. Although some prefer to train with variable resistance apparatus, others would rather use conventional weights. As will be discussed in greater detail in Chapter Four, there are definite advantages to training on variable resistance machines, but there are several reasons free weights should not be overlooked as a viable means of strength development. Regardless of the type of equipment with which one trains, there are certain principles of strength training that must be followed in order to attain optimum muscular development. These guidelines for safe and effective strength training are presented in the following chapter.

Chapter Three

Principles of Strength Training

People participate in weight training programs for many reasons, but predominant among these is a desire for larger and stronger muscles. Although the degree of muscular attainment is influenced by certain inherited factors such as somatotype, limb length, muscle length, angle of tendon insertion, and percentage of fast-twitch and slow-twitch muscle fibers, most people can achieve marked increases in muscle strength and hypertrophy through a systematic and progressive program of weight training. Research indicates that proper training results in the following adaptations within the muscular system: a higher concentration of contractile proteins, a greater number of myofibrils per muscle fiber, a greater number of capillaries per muscle fiber, an increased amount of connective tissue, a larger percentage of muscle fibers available for force production, and more efficient energy utilization.

There is no question that people who have engaged in widely varying programs of strength training have experienced muscular gains. Promoters of particular systems of strength augmentation are quick to point out how many champions their programs have produced. Far less publicized is the fact that strict adherence to many of these training regimens often results in muscle injury, strength decrement, and discouragement. The truth is, regardless of the training program one follows, the probability of experiencing desirable training consequences is closely related to the number of basic training principles observed by the exerciser. Conversely, the probability of encountering undesirable training consequences is closely related to the number of basic training principles violated by the exerciser.

A well-designed weight training program should incorporate the following fundamental principles of muscle development to insure gradual improvement in strength and to reduce the risk of tissue injury: Principle of Stress Adaptation, Principle of Rebuilding Time, Principle of Near-Maximum Resistance, Principle of Controlled Movement Speed, Principle of Full-Range Movements, Principle of Muscle Balance, and Principle of Training Specificity. While it is not the purpose of this chapter to compare different systems of muscle training, one rather unusual program will be presented to illustrate certain principles of muscle development that contribute to optimal training effectiveness.

It is reported that in ancient Greece, Milo of Crotona initiated an Olympic Games by carrying a full grown bull across the stadium. The training program that Milo used to accomplish this incredible feat of strength was very simple. Every day, beginning with the day the bull was born, he lifted the bull onto his shoulders and ran across the barnyard. While not the most sophisticated method of strength augmentation, Milo's training program satisfied some of the principles of muscle development and led to the achievement of his training objective.

PRINCIPLE OF STRESS ADAPTATION

When a muscle is stressed beyond its normal demands, it reacts in some way to that stress. If the stress is slightly greater than normal, the muscle responds positively and becomes stronger. That is, after a temporary decrease in ability following the training session, the muscle quickly rebuilds to a higher level of strength. On the other hand, if the imposed stress is too great the muscle reacts negatively and tissue damage results. For instance, if one hoes the garden for five minutes on Monday, ten minutes on Tuesday, fifteen minutes on Wednesday, and so on, the hands will gradually become calloused and hoeing can be continued for long periods of time without skin discomfort. However, if one begins by hoeing the garden for two hours on Monday, blisters are likely to develop and hoeing will have to be discontinued for several days until the skin heals. The phenomenon that occurs beneath the skin is actually quite similar. The person who progressively increases the intensity or duration of gardening activity will gradually condition the muscles involved, but the person who does too much too soon will experience muscle deconditioning during the several days required for the repair of damaged tissues.

The muscles respond to the stress of a weight training session in the same manner. If the intensity of the workout is increased gradually, the muscles respond positively and gain strength. However, if the intensity of the workout is increased abruptly, the muscles react negatively and tissue damage is likely to occur.

Example

Milo of Crotona trained his muscles in strict accordance with the Stress Adaptation Principle. Each day that Milo went to the barnyard he found his prize bull slightly heavier than the day before. These small daily increments in weightload provided the ideal training stimulus for Milo's muscles, gradual and progressive stress adaptation. It is important to note that Milo did not pick up a baby bull one day and a yearling the next day. Instead, he demonstrated a patient and controlled approach to strength training, which is the most effective way to promote injury-free muscle development.

Application

Strength training must be progressive. As soon as the muscle can accommodate a particular resistance, slightly greater stress should be applied to stimulate further strength improvement. Perhaps more important, large increments in resistance should be avoided. At best, disrespect for this training principle may result in chronic muscle fatigue and lack of progress. At worst, too much stress too soon may cause injury to muscle or connective tissue. Many people work as close to the breaking point as possible in an attempt to obtain their strength goals more quickly. Playing the edge may facilitate faster strength gains, but it is just as likely to lead to injury and frustration. It is better to set long-range goals and experience gradual improvement than to seek overnight results and spend many weeks rehabilitating injuries. Determining when to increase the training load is not really difficult. Each new workout should provide a clear indication as to whether the current weightload is too heavy, too light, or just about right. Observing a simple rule of not increasing the resistance of any exercise by more than 5 percent per week should insure sensible and safe progression.

PRINCIPLE OF REBUILDING TIME

When a muscle is stressed beyond its normal demands, a certain amount of time is required for the tissues to recover and make positive physiological adaptations. If the time between workouts is too short, the muscle is unable to rebuild to a higher level of strength before

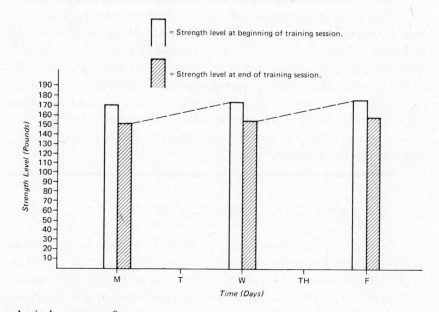

Figure 3–1 Hypothetical pattern of muscle response when recovery period is appropriate with respect to training intensity. When sufficient rest is obtained between training sessions, the muscle rebuilds to a slightly higher level of strength.

being stressed again. The cumulative effects of insufficient rebuilding time are chronically fatigued muscles that actually decrease in strength. Conversely, if the non-training interval is too long, the muscle will not maintain its strength gains, but will gradually return to its original level of contractile force.

Because the length of the rest interval depends on the intensity of the work interval, more hours are required for muscle rebuilding following a long workout than after a short workout. Each person must experimentally determine the optimal duration between workouts for his or her particular training program. Figure 3–1 schematically illustrates that the contractile force of a muscle decreases during a training session due to the stress imposed on it, but increases to a slightly higher strength level during a recovery period of sufficient duration.

As indicated in Figure 3–2, when too little rest is obtained between

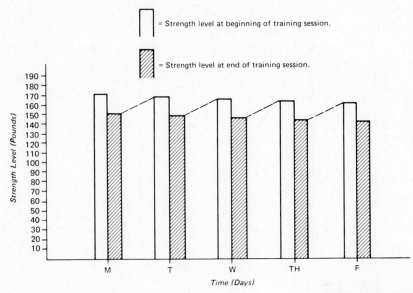

Figure 3–2 Hypothetical pattern of muscle response when recovery period is too short with respect to training intensity. When too little rest is obtained between training sessions, the muscle is unable to rebuild to a higher level of strength.

training sessions, the muscle is unable to rebuild to a higher level of strength prior to the next workout. The cumulative stress of repeated training sessions without sufficient time for muscle rebuilding leads to chronic training fatigue, and the muscles actually become weaker rather than stronger.

When too much rest is taken between successive workouts, the muscle initially rebuilds to a higher level of strength, but gradually returns to its original strength level prior to the next training session. Because the new strength level is not maintained indefinitely, it is important that the subsequent training stimulus occur near the top of the rebuilding curve. Taking too much rest between training sessions is not harmful, but the lack of strength gains can be frustrating. The consequences of an extended recovery period are illustrated schematically in Figure 3–3.

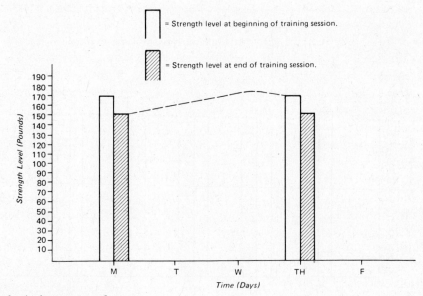

Figure 3–3 Hypothetical pattern of muscle response when recovery period is too long with respect to training intensity. When too much rest is taken between training sessions, the muscle initially rebuilds to a slightly higher level of strength, but gradually returns to its original strength level.

Example

It is reported that Milo of Crotona performed only one training task per day, that of hoisting the bull onto his shoulders and running across the barnyard. We may also assume that Milo, a member of the privileged society, did not engage in other exhausting work which would interfere with his recovery processes. Under these training conditions, Milo's 24-hour rest period was apparently adequate, and perhaps optimal, for muscle rebuilding and positive strength adaptations to take place.

Application

Weight training programs must insure sufficient rebuilding time between workout sessions to enable the muscles to attain higher strength levels. A decrease in performance generally indicates a need for more rest rather than a need for more work. Almost without exception, persons who begin a strength training program are eager to attain their goals and set out to do so in a hurry. Unfortunately, these good intentions often result in insufficient rest between workouts, which prohibits full recovery and maintains the muscles in a fatigued state. In addition to being a source of discouragement, fatigued muscles are highly susceptible to injury, particularly when worked harder in an attempt to force improvement.

Research findings indicate a direct relationship between the length of the training session and the duration of the recovery period. Westcott (1974) studied the relationship between the number of repetitions per training session and the number of training sessions per week when utilizing 5RM and 6RM workloads in the bench press exercise over a 7½ week training period. The term 5RM is an abbreviation for five repetitions maximum and refers to the heaviest weightload that one can lift five times in succession. The 6RM represents the heaviest weight-load that one can lift six times in succession.

As shown in Table 3–1, each training group performed a total of 60 repetitions per week. The number of repetitions per workout varied inversely with the number of workouts per week, so that the length of the recovery period was proportional to the length of the training session. The group that completed 60 bench presses per workout trained only

Table 3–1 Comparison of Four Strength Training Programs with Inverse Relationships between Length and Frequency of Training Sessions

Number of Reps Per Training Session	Number of Training Sessions Per Week	Total Number of Reps Per Week	Average Strength Increase (%/wk)
12 (2 sets, 6 reps)	5	60	2.9
20 (4 sets, 5 reps)	3	60	3.1
30 (6 sets, 5 reps)	2	60	2.2
60 (12 sets, 5 reps)	1	60	2.6

once each week. The subjects that executed 30 bench presses each workout trained twice a week. The group that performed 20 bench presses per session trained 3 times per week, and the subjects that did only 12 bench presses per workout trained 5 days a week.

Analyses of the results revealed that there were no statistically significant differences among the four training programs. All of the groups gained muscular strength at rates between 2.2 and 3.1 percent per week. This finding indicated that the relationship between the length of the training session and the length of the recovery period is an important factor in strength development, and one that can be accommodated to the personal training preference of the exerciser. Generally speaking, a short training session should be followed by a short recovery period, a medium length training session should be followed by a medium length recovery period, and a long training session should be followed by a long recovery period. The optimal length of the recovery period for a particular training program must be determined individually through trial and error procedures. However, one should realize that increasing the difficulty of one's workout routine may require a corresponding adjustment in rebuilding time to ensure continued strength improvement.

PRINCIPLE OF NEAR-MAXIMUM RESISTANCE

There are basically two ways to apply stress to one's muscles. One may perform numerous repetitions against low resistance (e.g., jogging, cycling, rope jumping, calisthenics) to improve muscular endurance, or one may perform few repetitions against high resistance (e.g., lifting heavy weights) to improve muscular strength. Each type of training stimulus produces specific results. If one's objective is to develop muscular strength and hypertrophy, the training program should focus on few repetitions with heavy weights.

Weight training authorities generally agree that weightloads exceeding 75 percent of maximum are most effective for promoting strength gains, because the single most important factor in strength development is the intensity of the training stimulus. Regardless of one's maximum weightload in a given exercise, the 10RM weightload usually corresponds to about 75 percent of that maximum. In other words, the heaviest weightload that one can lift ten times in succession is approximately 75 percent of the maximum weightload one can lift once.

Consequently, persons who train with 10RM weightloads apply sufficient muscular stress to produce strength improvement. Weightloads less than 75 percent of maximum are not as useful for strength augmentation, while weightloads greater than 75 percent of maximum may be somewhat more effective for developing muscular strength.

The principle of near-maximum resistance is often referred to as the *overload* principle because strength gains are dependent upon weightloads over and above those routinely encountered in one's daily activities. Because a true muscle overload would prevent the muscle from contracting concentrically, *near-maximum resistance* is a more accurate description of this training phenomenon.

Example

By performing a single lift with a heavy resistance (the bull), Milo insured that his muscles would be subjected to an adequate training stimulus for strength development. However, Milo was probably playing too close to the edge for comfort. Executing a single lift with maximal resistance is more appropriate for demonstrating strength than for building strength. Using the heaviest resistance possible for every workout is a dangerous practice, particularly when the weightload is wearing horns.

Application

The recommended number of repetitions for promoting optimum gains in strength varies from one to ten per set. When performing a single lift with maximum poundage, one always runs the risk of failure, discouragement, and tissue injury. On the other hand, if one executes more than ten repetitions per set a relatively light resistance must be used which necessarily reduces the stimulus for strength development. As indicated by Westcott's (1974) research findings (see Table 3–1), sets of five or six repetitions each appear to produce desirable rates of strength incrementation. Research studies performed by Dr. Richard Berger (1962*b,c*) also demonstrated that three sets of six repetitions each (6RM weightload) is an excellent training prescription for improving muscular strength.

PRINCIPLE OF CONTROLLED MOVEMENT SPEED

When training with weights, it is important to raise and lower the weightload in a slow and controlled manner to provide for consistent application of force throughout the exercise movement. Such a movement subjects the muscles to a more or less steady stress during both the lifting phase (concentric contraction) and the lowering phase (eccentric contraction). Experiments with force plates have revealed that lifting movements performed at a moderate speed require a relatively even application of muscular force. On the other hand, executing fast repetitions with a barbell or dumbbell is equivalent to throwing the weight. It seems that fast movements demand excessive muscular force at the beginning of the lift, but practically no muscle force is necessary during the midrange of the lift. Tests have demonstrated that during explosive lifting movements the exerciser is actually lifted by the weights. In fact, electronic traces of a quick press with a 60-pound barbell show a range of forces from over 100 pounds at the start of the lift to less than zero during the middle part of the lift. There can be little doubt that rapidly accelerating or decelerating a weightload subjects the muscles to widely varying levels of stress. Consequently, this type of training appears to be less productive in terms of strength development, and more likely to cause tissue injury.

It should also be recalled that intensity is the key to strength development. As the speed of movement increases, however, the weightload must necessarily be reduced. Consequently, weightloads that are light enough to permit rapid movements are less effective for promoting strength gains. One can train with light loads and fast repetitions or with heavy loads and slow repetitions, but the person interested in developing muscular strength is encouraged to use the latter method. Controlled lifting movements with relatively heavy weightloads are basic to safe and effective strength training programs.

Example

It is assumed that Milo treated his prize bull carefully, neither throwing the bull overhead nor dropping him abruptly to the ground. By lifting and lowering the bull in a slow, controlled manner, Milo prevented injury to both himself and the bull. He also provided his muscles with a greater stimulus for strength development.

Application

Weightlifting movements should be performed with a steady application of force. This applies to both the lowering phase and the lifting phase of the movement since the same muscles are involved in both aspects of the exercise. Fast movements are by no means recommended for improving muscular strength. If the movement can be performed rapidly, the resistance is probably not adequate to promote optimal strength adaptations. Generally speaking, the lifting movement (concentric contraction) should take about 1½ seconds and the lowering movement (eccentric contraction) should take about twice as long, approximately 3 seconds. In other words, it should take about 45 seconds to complete 10 repetitions with a 10RM weightload.

PRINCIPLE OF FULL-RANGE MOVEMENTS

When a muscle is exercised through a full range of motion there is little chance of decreasing joint flexibility. However, when opposing muscle groups are not exercised, or when partial movements are performed, there is a possibility of restricting one's range of joint mobility. For instance, it is not uncommon for a person desiring to bulk up the biceps to perform "cheat" curls in such a way that the arms remain partially flexed throughout the exercise. Such a practice could eventually lead to larger, shorter biceps muscles which might hinder full elbow extension. This undesirable outcome would be even more probable if the exerciser did not execute full-range movements for the antagonistic muscle group, the triceps.

Full-range movements also provide the muscles with a greater training stimulus, because the distance over which a muscle moves a weightload is proportional to the amount of work done:

$$Work = Force \times Distance$$

Consequently, the muscle that moves a weightload over a complete range of motion performs more work than the muscle that executes a partial movement with the same weightload. Full-range movements are, therefore, beneficial in terms of both flexibility development and strength development. Finally, since most athletic skills require application of force over the maximum distance possible (e.g., throwing, striking, kicking), performing less than full-range exercise movements has limited practical value.

Example

Assuming that Milo performed his daily exercise task by squatting beneath the bull, placing the bull squarely on his shoulders, and gradually rising to an erect position, he probably achieved full range of motion in his knee extensor muscles. It is doubtful, however, that he exercised his hip extensor muscles or back extensor muscles through a full range of motion. Lack of strength and flexibility in these muscle groups is often a contributing factor to lower back pain. Also, unless Milo proceeded to press the bull overhead, the involvement of his shoulder muscles was largely isometric. Milo's training program was highly specific and geared toward attaining a rather unusual objective. However, if he had understood the importance of full-range movements he might have performed some supplemental training exercises to maintain his flexibility and facilitate his strength development.

Application

Whenever possible, exercises that incorporate a full range of movement should be utilized. Specifically, triceps and biceps exercises should ensure maximum elbow extension and maximum elbow flexion for each repetition. Due to the hinge characteristics of the knee joint it is particularly important that knee extensor (quadriceps) exercises be performed to complete extension. If full knee extension cannot be obtained, the resistance is probably too heavy and should be reduced. It is almost always better to execute full-range movements with less resistance than to perform partial movements with greater resistance.

There are some muscle groups that are difficult to exercise through a full range of motion with conventional barbells. For example, most leg exercises do not provide full-range movement for the knee flexors (hamstrings). In order to strengthen this important and injury-prone muscle group, one should perform full-range leg curls on an appropriate apparatus. One of the advantages of Nautilus machines is that they are specifically designed to provide full-range exercise movements. (See Chapter Five, Strength Training Equipment.)

PRINCIPLE OF MUSCLE BALANCE

Weight training programs should be designed to promote strength development in all of the major muscle groups. Emphasizing certain muscle groups can produce muscle imbalance which may, in time, lead to muscle injury. Too often, athletes and weightlifters perform strengthening exercises only for the muscles that are prime movers in their particular event or activity. For example, sprinters and jumpers typically perform several strengthening exercises for their quadriceps muscles but few, if any, strengthening exercises for their hamstring muscles. This often results in an overpowering quadriceps group and a relatively weak hamstring group, which becomes highly susceptible to injury. The same problem is encountered by throwers who deliberately strengthen their triceps muscles but ignore their biceps and by competitive power-lifters who execute numerous sets of bench presses, incline presses, and other chest strengthening exercises without performing corresponding exercises for their back muscles.

Whenever a muscle group is disproportionately stronger than its antagonist, the latter is predisposed to injury. This is not to say that paired muscle groups should be trained to exactly equal strength. For example, the larger quadriceps muscles should be about 50 percent stronger than the smaller hamstring muscles. In other words, one would expect to use 50 percent more weight for a knee extension exercise such as leg extensions than for a knee flexion exercise such as leg curls. (See Chapter Six).

The important point is that the muscle groups should not be trained in isolation. If the muscles on one side of a joint are worked, then the muscles on the opposite side of the joint should likewise be worked, even though the training intensity would be reduced proportionately.

The problem of maintaining desirable muscle balance can be simplified by training all of the major muscle groups. (See Chapter Four.) This would require at least one exercise for each of the following muscle groups: chest, back, shoulders, triceps, biceps, midsection, quadriceps, hamstrings, lower legs, and forearms. Furthermore, one should not work the wrist extensors without also training the wrist flexors or the calf muscles apart from the shin muscles.

The Principle of Muscle Balance is a necessary counterpart to the Principle of Training Specificity. Training Specificity implies that one should exercise the particular muscle groups that one wants to strengthen. In other words, if one wants to improve in the bench press, then one should emphasize training exercises that strengthen those muscles involved in bench pressing. However, it appears that overly specialized training has been at least partially responsible for numerous injuries to muscle and connective tissue. The extra time and effort necessary to train one's muscles in a comprehensive and balanced manner seems to provide substantial dividends in terms of injury prevention and overall muscular development.

Example

Since Milo both lifted the bull up and set the bull down, he exercised most of his major muscle groups, right? No, the same muscles were used concentrically during the lifting phase and eccentrically during the lowering phase. That is, by increasing the number and rate of motor units firing in the quadriceps muscles, Milo was able to gradually extend his knees and lift the bull off the ground. Conversely, by decreasing the number and rate of motor units firing in the quadriceps muscles, Milo was able to gradually flex his knees and lower the bull gently back to earth. It is important to note that it was the gradual increase and decrease of muscle tension in the quadriceps that allowed Milo to both lift and lower the bull. The force of gravity is all that is needed to lower a weightload. Therefore, the same muscles that contracted concentrically to lift the weightload must act eccentrically to keep the weightload from dropping too quickly and causing injury.

This being the case, Milo apparently violated the principle of muscle balance. Unless he also performed exercises for the opposing (antagonist) muscle groups, he was developing strength disproportionately, which may have caused him pains and problems that are not recounted in the story.

Application

Regardless of specific training objectives, one should include exercises for all of the major muscle groups when designing a training program. Symmetrical and proportionate development of one's musculature sets a firm foundation for further strength improvement and minimizes the risk of injury to muscle and connective tissue.

Maintaining relative balance between opposing muscle groups is particularly important for preventing injuries. As previously indicated, the predisposing factor in a large percentage of hamstring pulls is muscle imbalance between a relatively strong quadriceps group and a relatively weak hamstrings group. It is, therefore, important to train the antagonistic muscle groups along with the prime mover groups. Well-trained antagonist muscles complement strong prime mover muscles, reducing the probability of injury and enhancing the quality of performance.

PRINCIPLE OF TRAINING SPECIFICITY

The Principle of Training Specificity relates to several aspects of strength development. As previously indicated, Training Specificity implies that one should diligently exercise the muscle groups one wants to strengthen. This requires a knowledge of both muscle function and exercise selection. For example, a gymnast who desires to perform an iron cross on the still rings should understand that the latissimus muscles of the back and the pectoralis muscles of the chest are primarily responsible for executing this difficult movement. The gymnast should then select those exercises that are most effective for strengthening these muscle groups (e.g., lat bar pull-downs, bench presses, pull-overs). The gymnast who trains with standing presses and barbell curls, two popular exercises that require only a barbell, will strengthen the shoulders and biceps muscles, but will not enhance the strength of the muscles that maintain the iron cross position.

Training specificity also means that the training program should accomplish one's training objectives. For example, people who desire to increase muscular strength should train with relatively heavy resistance and few repetitions. On the other hand, if one is interested in developing muscular endurance, the training program should involve relatively light resistance and many repetitions. The gymnast who wants to perform an iron cross should realize that this is a strength feat of brief duration. Consequently, his or her training program should be strength oriented rather than endurance oriented. The gymnast who executes 3 sets of 50 pushups and 3 sets of 20 pull-ups is exercising the right muscle groups (i.e., chest and back), but is more likely to improve muscular endurance than muscular strength. Three sets of 5 bench presses with the 5RM weightload and 3 sets of 5 lat bar pull-downs with the 5RM weightload would be more effective for increasing the strength of the chest and back muscles.

A further application of the Training Specificity Principle must be approached carefully. In some cases, such as training for an iron cross, an exercise can be designed that utilizes the same movements as the event. One could design a training apparatus that closely simulates the iron cross movements actually performed on the still rings. (See Figure 3–4.) With such an apparatus the gymnast could slowly raise and lower the arms against resistance in exactly the same way he or she performs the iron cross.

The Training Specificity Principle does not mean, however, that one should necessarily duplicate an athletic event while moving a heavy resistance. Events in which speed and/or timing play an important role generally should not be performed with greater resistance. To do so alters the neuromuscular pattern of the movement and may actually hinder performance. For example, putting a 20-pound shot involves a slightly different neuromuscular pattern than putting a regulation 16-pound shot. Therefore, any improvement in strength that results from training with the heavier shot would probably be offset by undesirable changes in movement speed and technique. When one goes back to the 16-pound shot for competition it will of course feel lighter, but

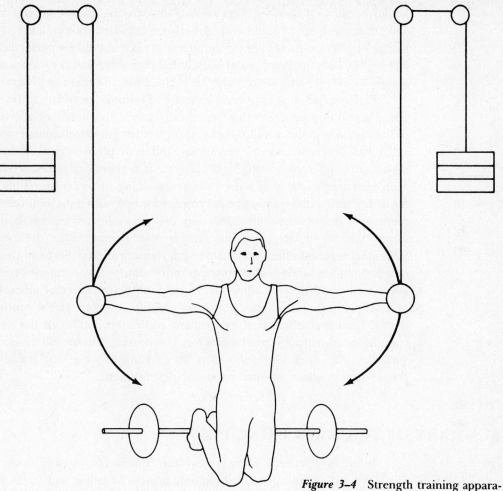

Figure 3–4 Strength training apparatus that simulates the movements used in performing an iron cross on the still rings.

the previous speed of movement and smoothness of movement is likely to be missing and the performance may be poorer than expected.

When dealing with dynamic athletic events (e.g., batting, throwing, kicking, jumping, etc.), the Training Specificity Principle is best applied by practicing the movement exactly as it will be performed in competition (i.e., same speed, same resistance, etc.). Rather than duplicating the actual event with increased resistance, the specific muscle groups involved in the event should be identified and standard training exercises for which these muscles are prime mover groups should be performed. In keeping with the Principle of Muscle Balance, exercises for the antagonistic muscle groups should also be included in the training program.

Perhaps the most important aspect of Training Specificity is developing a training program that specifically meets the needs of a given individual. Everyone who embarks upon a strength development program has different training objectives, different physiological endowments, and different psychological factors. It is therefore necessary for each exerciser to develop a personalized training program based upon his or her individual training requirements for optimal strength development. It is not recommended that any two persons train in exactly the same manner. In fact, even different muscle groups within the same individual respond differently to strength training stimuli. Some muscles develop quickly while others develop more slowly. Some muscles need greater amounts of work while others respond better to lesser amounts of work. No one person can positively identify someone else's training needs. Each individual must experiment and determine his or her own training needs through trial and error. Discovering the specific training variables that work best for you is an exciting process that leads to the desired product, optimal muscular development.

SUMMARY OF TRAINING PRINCIPLES

In the final analysis, there are two fundamental features of an effective program of strength development, muscle isolation and stress intensification. Essentially, one singles out a specific muscle group and gradually applies greater and greater stress to it. There are three simple steps one should follow to train in this manner. First, one should identify a particular muscle group to be strengthened (e.g., triceps muscles). Second, one should select an exercise for which the target muscle group is a prime mover (e.g., triceps press-downs). Third, the exerciser must progressively increase the intensity of the training stimulus (e.g., increase the weightload by 5 percent when three sets of six repetitions each can be completed).

Given this basic framework for improving muscular strength, one should train in accordance with the Principles of Strength Development presented in this chapter. Adherence to these guidelines should increase the probability that muscle strength will be gained, that muscle balance will be maintained, and that muscle injury will be avoided.

The Principles of Stress Adaptation, Rebuilding Time, Near-Maximum Resistance, Controlled Movement Speed, Full-Range Movements, Muscle Balance, and Training Specificity apply to all persons and all training programs. However, each individual should employ these principles in the manner that is most effective for promoting his or her own strength development. For example, some persons will increase resistance more quickly than others, and some persons will recover more quickly than others. The important thing is that one's personal training program incorporate each of these training principles in a way that is compatible with his or her own physiological and psychological characteristics. "Know yourself and be yourself" is an excellent motto for successful and enjoyable strength training experiences.

Chapter Four

Designing the Exercise Program

EXERCISE SELECTION

A cursory look at almost any strength training text or popular strength magazine will reveal dozens of specialized exercises for most of the muscle groups in the human body. Depending on one's training objectives, some of these exercises will be more appropriate than others. Exercise selection is, therefore, an important aspect of one's training program, because the exercises utilized determine which muscle groups will be stressed and strengthened. The athlete concerned with leg strength would undoubtedly incorporate a different training routine than the athlete interested in upper body development.

Major Muscle Groups

For the person whose primary concern is overall and balanced muscular development, there are basically ten major muscle groups that should receive attention in the training program. These are: 1) chest,

2) back, 3) shoulders, 4) triceps, 5) biceps, 6) midsection, 7) quadriceps, 8) hamstrings, 9) lower legs, and 10) forearms. It would be an easy task to find ten or more different exercises for each of these muscle groups. Since few people have the time or inclination to perform all of the exercise variations, several factors should be taken into consideration when designing a personal exercise program.

Desired Outcomes

Perhaps the most important factor in designing the exercise program is the desired outcome. There are many reasons for beginning a strength training program. Athletes involved in contact sports frequently take up weight training in order to gain overall size and strength. Other athletes may be more concerned with specifically increasing their jumping power or upper body strength. Some people are interested in the sport of bodybuilding, while others want to become competitive weight-lifters or powerlifters. Often, persons begin a strength training program to increase their arm size or chest measurement. In many cases, the training objective is injury rehabilitation or improved muscle balance between opposing muscle groups. Whatever the reason for initiating a strength training program, the exerciser must first determine which muscle groups should be strengthened. The next step is to select those exercises which most effectively stress these muscle groups, that is, exercises for which these muscles are the prime movers. Finally, some exercises should be included for the opposing (antagonistic) muscle groups to promote muscle balance and to reduce the risk of muscle injury. (See Chapter Three, Principle of Muscle Balance.)

Availability of Training Equipment

Another factor that has a bearing on exercise selection is the availability of training equipment. For persons who have access to high school, college, or commercial training facilities this may be a minor problem, but for those who train at home, equipment resources are a major consideration when planning an exercise routine. Fortunately, there are enough exercise variations that an excellent overall training program can be carried out with rather limited equipment. For example, if lat bar pull-down apparatus is not available for back exercises, one might select weighted pull-ups as an alternative exercise. If a pull-up bar is also unavailable, the exerciser could choose to do bent rows using either a barbell or dumbbells. Because the latissimus muscles function as prime mover groups in all three of these exercises, lack of specialized equipment need not pose a serious threat to the development of one's back musculature. In Chapter Six, exercises are presented for each of the major muscle groups that can be performed with basic equipment, specialized equipment, and commercial exercise machines.

Type of Training Program

Exercise selection is also related to the training program one wishes to employ. For example, persons, such as powerlifters, who train with very heavy weights typically perform fewer exercises than persons, such as bodybuilders, who use moderately heavy resistance. Also, persons who execute several sets per exercise usually select fewer exercises than persons who perform few sets per exercise or train with paired exercises. The amount of time one has available for strength training is undoubtedly an important factor, but personal preference actually has a greater influence on exercise selection. Given thirty minutes of training time, there are those who would do one set each with ten different exercises, and others who would complete ten sets of a single exercise.

Exercise Variations

Decisions regarding exercise selection can be further complicated by examining the popular strength training literature. Every magazine issue reveals new training exercises and exercise variations for improved muscular development. For example, the following is a partial list of back exercises recommended by different strength experts for developing the latissimus dorsi muscles: 1) lat bar pull-down—wide grip, 2) lat bar pull-down—narrow grip, 3) lat bar pull-down—palms facing, 4) lat bar pull-down—palms away, 5) bent rows—wide grip, 6) bent rows—narrow grip, 7) bent rows—palms facing, 8) bent rows—palms away, 9) bent rows—hinged bar, 10) seated rows—wide grip, 11) seated rows—narrow grip, 12) seated rows—palms facing, 13) seated rows—palms away, 14) pull-ups—wide grip, 15) pull-ups—narrow grip, 16) pull-ups—palms facing, 17) pull-ups—palms away, 18) bent arm pull-overs, 19) straight arm pull-overs, and 20) bar dips. Many of these exercises can be performed with either dumbbells or barbells, and several can be done on different types of variable resistance equipment. In addition to these back exercises, other alternatives include springs, cables, wall pulleys, rope climbing, isometrics, and towel pulls with partners.

It becomes evident that one could spend the greater part of a day executing just those exercises recommended for a single muscle group. Is such quantity of training exercises necessary? Not really, and certainly not during any one training session. While frequent changes in the training routine are encouraged for the sake of variety, it is not necessary to perform more than two or three separate exercises per workout for a particular muscle group. After all, how one holds the lat bar or pull-up bar has little effect on the latissimus muscles. In both of these exercises the latissimus muscles function to bring the upper arms from an overhead position to a position along the sides of the body. This specific movement of the upper arms is a common action whether one uses a wide grip, narrow grip, palms facing grip, palms away grip, pulls a lat bar to the shoulders, or pulls the shoulders to a chinning bar. The latissimus muscles are prime movers for shoulder extension and shoulder adduction, and it is this basic movement, rather than the hand position, that produces tension in these muscles. The degree of tension that is developed in the latissimus muscles depends primarily on the magnitude of the resistance utilized in the exercise.

Choosing the Right Exercises

Let us assume that one of your training objectives is to increase the strength of the latissimus muscles. Let us further assume that you have decided to incorporate two different back exercises into your training program. Which ones should you select? This depends on several factors which can be most easily evaluated through the process of experimental elimination.

First, try out every back exercise for which equipment is available. Perform each exercise in a slow, controlled manner with attention to form, and to the degree of muscle tension developed during the exercise movement. Any exercise that produces pain or discomfort in or around the joints should be discarded immediately. For example, if a close-grip exercise causes strain in the wrists it should not be used. Tension should be felt in the target muscles and not in the joints. Also, any exercise that does not create a reasonable degree of tension in the target muscles is less likely to produce the desired results.

Second, eliminate any exercise that is tedious to perform. That is, do not include an exercise that you do not enjoy doing. The wide-grip pull-up is an excellent exercise for strengthening the latissimus muscles, but if for some reason you dislike this particular exercise then do not use it. No single exercise is critical to your progress. It is much more important that you enjoy performing every exercise in your training routine, and that you look forward to each training session. Obtaining the desired results is a key aspect of any exercise program, but enjoying the training process is absolutely essential.

Third, distinguish between those exercises that incorporate full-range movements and those that do not. Other things being equal, the exercise that moves the joint through a greater range of degrees should be preferred. It should be noted that every barbell exercise can also be performed with dumbbells. In many cases, dumbbell exercises provide a greater range of movement than their barbell counterparts. For example, due to the lower starting position, tension can be developed over a greater distance in the chest and shoulder muscles when dumbbells are used for the bench press exercise.

Fourth, remember that strength development is closely related to training intensity. (See Chapter Three, Principle of Near-Maximum Resistance.) Consequently, exercises that can be performed with relatively heavy weights should be chosen over those that require relatively light weights. As a general rule, straight arm exercises such as lateral raises, straight arm flies, and straight arm pull-overs should be selected as secondary rather than primary exercises, since relatively light weights must be used to execute these movements. In a similar manner, leg extensions and leg curls require considerably lighter weightloads than half squats and vertical leg presses, and should supplement rather than replace the latter exercises.

Fifth, it is probably better to use two distinctly different exercises than to perform variations of essentially the same movement. For example, wide-grip lat bar pull-downs and narrow-grip lat bar pull-downs provide almost identical training stimuli to the latissimus muscles. The same is true for wide and narrow grip pull-ups, wide and narrow grip bent rows, and most other exercises which employ assorted hand positions. Movements which begin and end in approximately the same positions generally incorporate the same stabilizer muscles. As these muscles become fatigued, the training intensity must be reduced even though the target muscles may not be maximally stressed. By choosing two exercises that are dissimilar in form, such as lat bar pull-downs and bent rows, one utilizes different stabilizer muscles and tends to reduce the cumulative effects of fatigue. Also, it seems psychologically easier to begin an exercise that does not closely resemble the previous exercise. Performing two variations of the same exercise often reduces one's enthusiasm and results in a less productive training session.

Sixth, it is recalled that muscular development is dependent upon progressive and systematic increases in resistance. (See Chapter Three, Stress Adaptation Principle.) Therefore, one should incorporate only those exercises that permit gradual and precise increments in resistance. This does not automatically rule out bodyweight exercises, such as pull-ups, bar dips, or situps. Resistance can be added in the first two exercises by attaching barbell plates to a rope slung over the hips. The degree of difficulty in the latter exercise can be easily varied by holding barbell plates behind the neck, placing the situp board on a steeper incline, or both. However, it is quite difficult to make small and precise increments in resistance when using springs, isometric exercises, and certain types of isokinetic devices. Ideally, dumbbell sets, barbell equipment, and variable resistance machines should permit weight increments of 2½ pounds. In many exercises, 5-pound increases are often too demanding and may lead to tissue injury. This is particularly true of dumbbell exercises such as flies, lateral raises, and seated curls. Keep in mind that a change from a 25-pound dumbbell to a 30-pound dumbbell represents a 20 percent increase in resistance and requires a corresponding increase in muscular tension.

Number of Exercises

Although there are ten major muscle groups that should be exercised, the manner in which one trains is by and large a matter of personal preference. Some individuals perform as many as 4 separate exercises for each muscle group, for a total of 40 different exercises. Competitive bodybuilders typically fit into this category, and often spend several hours a day in the weight training room.

Persons with different goals or fewer available training hours may prefer to do a limited number of exercises, each of which involves several major muscle groups. For example, the bench press, lat bar pull-down, and vertical leg press are a sufficient training routine to promote strength gains in most of the major muscle groups. (See Chapter Six for exercise descriptions and illustrations.) The bench press involves three major muscle groups, namely the chest, triceps, and anterior shoulders. The lat bar pull-down applies stress to the opposing muscle groups, namely the back, biceps, and posterior shoulders. In addition, both of these exercises produce isometric contractions in the forearm muscles. Therefore, between these two exercises, all of the major upper body muscle groups receive some training stimuli.

The three major muscle groups of the lower body are involved in the vertical leg press. The knee extension and hip extension required to perform the vertical leg press are produced by concentric contraction of the quadriceps and hamstring muscles, respectively. By extending the ankles (toe-lifts) at the top of the lifting movement, one can also stress the calf muscles of the lower legs. The only major muscle group not directly addressed by these three exercises is the midsection. Although the midsection muscles may function in a stabilizer role during the bench press and lat bar pull-down, it is difficult to adequately stress these muscles without performing some specific abdominal and lower back exercises.

The bench press, lat bar pull-down, and vertical leg press are usually performed with relatively heavy weightloads, and thereby provide the exerciser with a high intensity training program. It is interesting to note that many prominent bodybuilders and weightlifters spent the first year or two of their training programs on only three or four basic exercises.

Exercises on Universal Gym Equipment

Many people choose to follow a training program that consists of one exercise for each major muscle group. An exercise routine of this nature is particularly convenient if one has access to Universal Gym or Nautilus Sports equipment. Although there are many variations available, the following exercises are recommended for Universal Gym training (see Chapter Six for exercise descriptions and illustrations): 1) chest—bench press, 2) back—lat bar pull-down, 3) shoulders—upright rows, 4) triceps—press-down, 5) biceps—standing curl, 6) midsection—trunk curls on incline board, 7) quadriceps—leg extension, 8) hamstrings—leg curl, 9) lower legs—toe raises, 10) forearms—wrist rolls. Universal Gym equipment also includes an apparatus for training the neck muscles for those persons who wish to develop this muscle group.

Exercises on Nautilus Sports Equipment

Nautilus Sports Equipment also includes more than one piece of exercise apparatus for most major muscle groups. The following is a program of exercises that includes nine major muscle groups, as well as the neck muscles (see Chapter Six for exercise descriptions and illustrations): 1) chest—decline press and bent arm fly on the Double Chest Machine, 2) back—pull-over and lat bar pull-down on the Duo-Poly Pullover Machine, 3) shoulders—side lateral raise and seated press on the Double Shoulder Machine, 4) triceps—triceps extensions on the Biceps-Triceps Machine, 5) biceps—biceps curl on the Biceps-Triceps Machine, 6) quadriceps—leg extension and leg press on the Compound Leg Machine, 7) hamstrings—leg curl on the Leg Curl Machine, 8) lower legs—heel raise on the Multi-Exercise Machine, 9) forearms—wrist curl on the Multi-Exercise Machine, and 10) neck—neck extension and flexion on the Four-Way Neck Machine.

Exercises with Free Weights

For persons who prefer to train with free weights (barbells and dumbbells), the following exercises are recommended for the ten major muscle groups (see Chapter Six for exercise descriptions and illustrations): 1) chest—bench press, 2) back—bent rows, 3) shoulders—upright rows, 4) triceps—triceps extension, 5) biceps—standing curl, 6) midsection—trunk curls with barbell plate behind the neck, 7) quadriceps—half squat, 8) hamstrings—half squat, 9) lower legs—toe raises, and 10) forearms—wrist rolls. The equipment necessary to perform the exercises in this training program includes a flat exercise bench and a pair of adjustable barbell supports.

Paired Exercises

Perhaps the most important aspect of exercise selection is the proper pairing of exercises. To promote muscle balance, flexibility, and injury-free training one should exercise both prime mover muscles and antagonist muscles. For example, it is a good practice to pair a biceps exercise (e.g., standing curl) with a triceps exercise (e.g., triceps pressdown). Likewise, one should complement a quadriceps exercise (e.g., leg extension) with a hamstring exercise (e.g., leg curl). Although some leg exercises involve both the quadriceps and hamstrings groups (e.g., half squat, vertical leg press), it is nonetheless advisable to include some leg curls and leg extensions, if possible, to ensure balanced leg development. Finally, because many people favor the bench press exercise, they tend to develop powerful chest and anterior shoulder muscles which pull the shoulder girdle forward and give a round-shouldered appearance. It is therefore recommended that the bench press exercise be paired with an exercise for the back and posterior shoulder muscles, such as lat bar pull-downs, bent rows, or pull-ups to promote balanced muscle development in the shoulder girdle area.

EXERCISE SEQUENCE

Pairing exercises for prime mover and antagonistic muscle groups is an important aspect of sequencing exercises, but there are several other things that one should consider when designing a training sequence. Ordering one's exercises so that each muscle group receives maximum stimulation is an important aspect of an efficient and effective training program.

Larger Muscle Groups First

To begin with, it is most desirable to perform those exercises that use heavier weightloads early in the workout. These are the exercises that involve the larger muscle groups, such as the legs, chest, and back. Since these muscle groups are fundamental to overall strength development, it is important that they be trained while one is fresh and capable of handling relatively heavy weightloads. Consider what might occur if one waited until the end of a workout session to do bench presses.

Example

John normally begins his training session with three sets of bench presses at 200 pounds. Later in the training program he does three sets of triceps press-downs with 65 pounds. One day John reverses his training sequence. Although he can now handle 75 pounds in the triceps press-downs, he finds he must drop down to 175 pounds for his bench presses. Because his triceps have already received a stressful workout in the press-down exercise, they are too fatigued to complete 3 sets of bench presses at 200 pounds. Under these circumstances 175 pounds feels heavy and provides near-maximum stress for the already tired triceps muscles. However, the reduced bench press weightload is not sufficient to promote optimal development of John's chest and shoulder muscles, and is therefore detrimental to his overall progress. It is better to perform the multi-muscle exercise first, and then move to the single-muscle exercise. Using less weight in the triceps press-down exercise does not jeopardize any other muscle groups, and still provides near-maximum stress for the previously worked triceps.

Alternate Muscle Groups

In addition to exercising the larger muscle groups first, it is recommended that the same muscle groups not be required to perform successive exercises. Muscle groups that are alternately stressed and rested partially recover from their first exercise and are able to handle relatively greater weightloads in the second exercise. Since strength development is closely related to training intensity, one should obtain better strength gains when exercises that involve a particular muscle group are alternated with exercises that do not stress that muscle group.

Example

The triceps muscles are prime movers in both the bench press and triceps press-down exercises. John finds that when he performs triceps press-downs immediately after doing bench presses he can handle 65 pounds in the latter exercise. On the other hand, when John does standing curls (biceps exercise) between bench presses and triceps press-downs he is able to use 70 pounds for his press-downs. In both cases, John's triceps muscles are in a state of fatigue following the bench press workout, and are therefore unable to produce maximum force. However, when a non-triceps exercise is performed after the bench press, the triceps muscles have time to partially recover and are able to accommodate relatively greater resistance in the press-down exercise. Although there are some instances in which one might intentionally execute successive exercises for the same muscle groups, strength development is enhanced when the recovery period is sufficient to permit the use of near-maximum resistance.

Recommended Exercise Sequences

The following are recommended sequences of exercises with attention to training the larger muscle groups first and alternating exercises for particular muscle groups. The exercises are also paired with respect to prime mover and antagonist muscle groups to facilitate balanced strength development.

Training Program Involving One Exercise for Each Major Muscle Group

Exercise	Prime Mover Muscle Group	
Bench Press	Chest, triceps, anterior shoulders	} Paired
Lat Bar Pull-down	Back, biceps, posterior shoulders	
Upright Row	Shoulders, trapezius	} Paired
Triceps Press-down	Triceps	
Standing Curl	Biceps	} Paired
Leg Extension	Quadriceps	
Leg Curl	Hamstrings	} Paired
Abdominal Curls	Abdominals	
Hyperextensions	Lower back	} Paired
Toe Raises	Lower leg anterior (shin muscles)	
Heel Raises	Lower leg posterior (calf muscles)	} Paired
Wrist Curls	Forearm flexors	
Wrist Extensions	Forearm extensors	} Paired

Training Program Involving Two Exercises for Each Major Muscle Group

Exercise	Prime Mover Muscle Group	
Vertical Leg Press	Quadriceps, hamstrings	
Bench Press	Chest, triceps, anterior shoulders	} Paired
Lat Bar Pull-down	Back, biceps, posterior shoulders	
Upright Rows	Shoulders, trapezius	} Paired
Leg Extension	Quadriceps	
Leg Curl	Hamstrings	} Paired
Incline Press	Chest, triceps, anterior shoulders	} Paired
Bent Row	Back, biceps, posterior shoulders	
Lateral Raises	Shoulders, trapezius	} Paired
Triceps Press-down	Triceps	
Standing Curl	Biceps	} Paired

Abdominal Curl	Abdominals	} Paired
Hyperextensions	Lower back	
French Dumbbell Press	Triceps	} Paired
Seated Dumbbell Curl	Biceps	
Bent Knee Situp	Abdominals	} Paired
Good Morning	Lower back	
Toe Raises	Lower leg anterior (shin muscles)	} Paired
Heel Raises	Lower leg posterior (calf muscles)	
Wrist Curls	Forearm flexor muscles	} Paired
Wrist Extensions	Forearm extensor muscles	

EXERCISE SPEED

The speed at which one performs an exercise is inversely related to the intensity of the exercise. That is, as the exercise resistance (weightload) increases, the exercise speed necessarily decreases. Conversely, as the exercise resistance decreases, the exercise speed can be increased.

One can easily demonstrate the relationship between weightload and exercise speed by performing the following experiment. Using an unloaded barbell, execute ten bench presses as quickly as possible while someone records the time. Add 20 pounds and again execute ten bench presses as fast as you can while someone records the time. Repeat this procedure until you reach the heaviest weightload that you can lift ten times in succession (10RM weightload). You will note that as more weight is added, more time is required to complete the ten repetitions. This demonstrates that as the exercise intensity increases, the exercise speed decreases, and vice versa. Figure 4–1 illustrates a typical speed-intensity curve for performing ten repetitions with various weightloads in the bench press exercise.

The principle of training specificity indicates that one can train for strength by using relatively heavy resistance, or one can train for speed by utilizing relatively light resistance. It should be understood, however, that training with fast, explosive repetitions does not necessarily increase the speed of other movements, or even of similar movements performed with less resistance.

For example, one can simulate the shot putting movement by performing incline dumbbell presses. Furthermore, one can execute repetitions more quickly with 20-pound dumbbells than with 60-pound dumb-

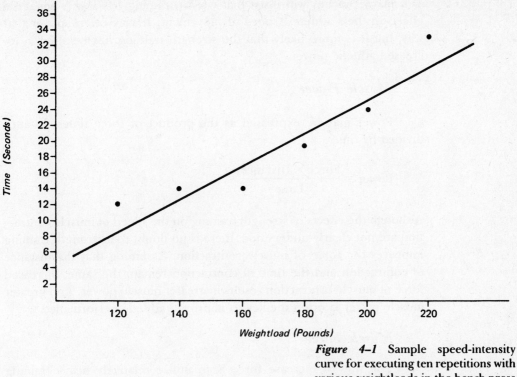

Figure 4–1 Sample speed-intensity curve for executing ten repetitions with various weightloads in the bench press exercise. Note that as the weightload increases, the repetitions are performed more slowly.

bells. One cannot, however, move a 20-pound dumbbell as fast as one can move a 16-pound shot. Therefore, contrary to popular belief, fast repetitions with 20-pound dumbbells do not increase one's arm speed in the shot put. In order to practice the shot putting action at a faster speed one must use a resistance that is less than 16 pounds. Because the shot put is a complex action involving precision timing and the synchronous contraction of several major muscle groups, it would be better to practice the actual putting motion with a 12-pound shot than to do incline presses with a 12-pound dumbbell.

Unless a weight training exercise actually duplicates a particular sports skill, it is unlikely to improve the speed of that specific movement. As any sprint coach can verify, it is difficult to improve one's movement speed, because speed is primarily determined by neurological factors.

Yet, many coaches will insist that weight training has had a beneficial effect on their athletes' speed of movement. It may often appear that way, but it is more likely that the strength training has resulted in increased athletic power.

Muscle Power

Power may be expressed as the product of force times distance divided by time.

$$\text{Power} = \frac{\text{Force} \times \text{Distance}}{\text{Time}}$$

Although the effects of strength training on the speed of muscle contraction are not clearly understood, there is no doubt that strength training improves the force of muscle contraction. Assuming that the distance of contraction and the time of contraction remain the same, increased force of muscle contraction results in greater muscle power. And greater muscle power is often the key to improved athletic performance.

Muscle Force

The way to increase force is to utilize relatively heavy training loads, which necessarily require relatively slow repetitions. Weightlifting movements should be characterized by a steady application of force during both the lowering phase (eccentric contraction) and the lifting phase (concentric contraction). Rapid repetitions preclude the use of weightloads that are heavy enough to promote maximum gains in strength. It is also doubtful that the actual movement speed of most athletic events can be improved through strength training regardless of the exercise speed. The purpose of strength training is to increase muscular strength, which in turn produces greater muscular power. Because muscle power is essential for the successful performance of most athletic events, strength training can be highly beneficial to athletes. Muscle strength and power are most likely to improve when the training load is relatively heavy (10RM or greater) and when each repetition takes about 4½ seconds to complete. Consequently, fast repetitions with light weightloads are of little practical value in a strength training program.

RESISTANCE

Resistance is the key to strength development. Regardless of the number of sets and repetitions one performs, strength will not be augmented unless the resistance is sufficient to stimulate strength-related adaptations within the muscles. As discussed in Chapter Three, muscular strength is effectively increased by performing few repetitions with relatively heavy weightloads. This is referred to as a high-intensity training program. Executing numerous repetitions with relatively light weights improves muscular endurance but does not result in greater muscular strength. Training in this manner is characteristic of a low-intensity program.

There is little agreement as to what constitutes a heavy weightload. Some strength training authorities recommend the heaviest weightload that the exerciser can lift 12 times in succession (12RM weightload), while others advocate the heaviest weightload that can be lifted 6 times in succession (6RM weightload). Still others believe that one should train with the heaviest weightload possible (1RM weightload) on a regular basis to promote maximum strength gains.

Even the research regarding effective weightloads is somewhat inconclusive. Hettinger (1961) reported strength increases when muscles were isometrically trained at 50 percent of their maximum contractile force. However, Berger (1965) found no strength improvement when the training resistance was 67 percent of the maximum weightload in the squat exercise.

In terms of strength development, one lift with a maximum weightload (e.g., 1×300 lbs.) is more productive than 3 lifts with one-third of the maximum weightload (e.g., 3×100 lbs.), even though the total amount of weight lifted is the same in both cases. In fact, even 10, 15, or 20 repetitions with one-third of the maximum weightload will not promote strength gains because the training intensity is simply insufficient to stimulate positive strength adaptations. This would be analogous to a sprinter running repeat 100 meters at one-third intensity (i.e., 30 seconds each) to improve speed. On the other hand, it is psychologically difficult to gear up for a maximum performance during every workout. This would be similar to running one's best time in the 100 meters every training session. Consequently, most people train with weightloads that are slightly less than maximal. As a generalization, it is safe to say that a typical training resistance is between 70 and 95 percent of one's maximum weightload. Weightloads less than 70 percent of maximum do not provide sufficient stress for optimal strength development, and weightloads greater than 95 percent of maximum are probably too strenuous to deal with on an every workout basis.

REPETITIONS

There is an inverse relationship between the weightload utilized for a particular exercise and the number of repetitions that can be executed. When one uses the heaviest weightload possible, one is necessarily limited to a single lift. On the other hand, the more the weightload is reduced the more repetitions one can perform.

Persons who train with weights generally ask two questions about weightloads and repetitions. How much weight should be used, and how many repetitions should be done? Actually the answer to the first question largely determines the answer to the second question, because one should generally perform as many repetitions as possible with a given weightload. If one chooses the heaviest weightload one can lift once, then, quite obviously, only one repetition can be performed. This is referred to as the one repetition maximum weightload (1RM weightload). If one chooses the heaviest weightload that can be lifted five times in succession, then five repetitions should be attempted. This is called the five repetition maximum weightload (5RM weightload). In a similar manner, if one selects the heaviest weightload that can be lifted ten times in a row, then ten repetitions should be attempted. This is referred to as the ten repetition maximum weightload (10RM weightload).

The 10RM Weightload

The 10RM weightload has long been a popular training resistance. Regardless of strength level, one's 10RM weightload is approximately 75 percent of one's 1RM weightload. For example, if Jim can perform a single bench press with 200 pounds, his 10RM weightload should be about 150 pounds. Likewise, if Sue's 1RM bench press is 100 pounds, her 10RM weightload should be about 75 pounds. The 10RM weightload is both heavy enough to promote strength development and light enough to allow about 45 seconds of vigorous exercise. (Remember that each repetition should take approximately 4½ seconds.)

The DeLorme-Watkins Program

The concept of the repetition maximum and the use of the 10RM weightload for training purposes was introduced by Thomas DeLorme and Arthur Watkins in the late 1940s. Their work with muscle rehabilitation produced one of the first systematic and progressive weight training programs to receive approval from both medical and physical education professionals. Their original strength training routine consisted of three exercise bouts, generally referred to as sets, of ten repetitions each. The first set of ten repetitions is performed with 50 percent of the 10RM weightload and serves as a first level warm-up set. The second set of ten repetitions is executed with 75 percent of the 10RM weightload and serves as a second level warm-up set. The final set of ten repetitions utilizes 100 percent of the 10RM weightload and is the actual stimulus for strength development.

Example

The heaviest weightload that John can press ten times in succession (10RM weightload) is 100 pounds. According to the DeLorme-Watkins training formula, John should do the following workout.

First Set: 10 repetitions with 50 pounds (50% 10RM weightload)
Second Set: 10 repetitions with 75 pounds (75% 10RM weightload)
Third Set: 10 repetitions with 100 pounds (100% 10RM weightload)

As John's muscles respond to the training stimulus he will be able to complete more than 10 repetitions with 100 pounds. DeLorme and Watkins recommended that a new 10RM weightload be established when the exerciser can perform 15 repetitions with the previous 10RM weightload. This ensures a gradual and progressive application of stress in accordance with the stress adaptation principle. This program actually represents what is often referred to as a double progressive training approach, because the exerciser alternately increases the number of repetitions and the exercise weightload.

Although the actual process of strength development is influenced by a variety of factors (see Chapter Two, Factors that Affect Strength), a typical response to the DeLorme-Watkins training program might resemble the hypothetical pattern of progression shown in Table 4–1. It should be noted that the DeLorme-Watkins approach incorporates an alternate day training schedule.

DeLorme and Watkins' program for strength development involves two warm-up sets and one set requiring maximum effort. The final set of ten repetitions with the 10RM weightload provides the essential training stimulus for positive strength adaptations to occur. Beginning in 1962, Richard Berger began to experiment with different combinations of sets and repetitions in an attempt to determine the most effective training program for improving muscular strength.

Table 4–1   Hypothetical Pattern of Progression in the Bench Press Exercise Using the DeLorme-Watkins Training Program

Week	Monday	Wednesday	Friday
1	60 lbs × 10	60 lbs × 10	60 lbs × 10
	90 lbs × 10	90 lbs × 10	90 lbs × 10
	120 lbs × 10	120 lbs × 11	120 lbs × 12
2	60 lbs × 10	60 lbs × 10	60 lbs × 10
	90 lbs × 10	90 lbs × 10	90 lbs × 10
	120 lbs × 12	120 lbs × 13	120 lbs × 13
3	60 lbs × 10	60 lbs × 10	60 lbs × 10
	90 lbs × 10	90 lbs × 10	90 lbs × 10
	120 lbs × 14	120 lbs × 13	120 lbs × 14
4	60 lbs × 10	60 lbs × 10	New 10RM
	90 lbs × 10	90 lbs × 10	found to be
	120 lbs × 14	120 lbs × 15	135 lbs
5	65 lbs × 10	65 lbs × 10	65 lbs × 10
	100 lbs × 10	100 lbs × 10	100 lbs × 10
	135 lbs × 10	135 lbs × 11	135 lbs × 11
6	65 lbs × 10	65 lbs × 10	65 lbs × 10
	100 lbs × 10	100 lbs × 10	100 lbs × 10
	135 lbs × 12	135 lbs × 13	135 lbs × 13

The Berger Program

One of Berger's first experiments dealt with the optimum number of repetitions one should perform when training with a single set. His findings indicated that one set of the 4RM, 6RM, or 8RM weightload produced greater strength gains than one set of the 2RM, 10RM, or 12RM weightload. He therefore concluded that training with three to nine repetitions encompassed the optimum number of repetitions for increasing strength when training with one set, three times weekly.

Because persons who train with weights typically perform more than one set of an exercise, Berger conducted several studies involving various combinations of sets and repetitions. His best known study (1962*b*) compared all combinations of one, two, and three sets with two, six, and ten repetitions per set. (See Table 4–2.) The results of this study suggested that three sets of six repetitions each with the 6RM weightload was the most effective training stimulus for gaining muscular strength. Although subsequent investigations by Berger (1963) and O'Shea (1966) did not confirm the superiority of this training program, three sets of six repetitions with the 6RM weightload has become a very popular training format, particularly for beginners and non-competitive weight trainers.

When one begins training with the 6RM weightload, one will probably execute fewer than six repetitions in the second and third sets due to the effects of fatigue. However, as strength increases, the exerciser will be able to complete six repetitions in all three sets. At that time the weightload should be increased by 5 percent and the strength building process begun anew. Although strength development is a phenomenon influenced by a number of factors (see Chapter Two, Factors that Affect Strength), a typical response to the Berger training program might resemble the hypothetical pattern of progression indicated in Table 4–3. It should be noted that the Berger system utilizes a three day per week training schedule.

Table 4–2 Combinations of Sets and Repetitions Studied by Berger for Effects on Strength Development

1 Set of 2RM	2 Sets of 2RM	3 Sets of 2RM
1 Set of 6RM	2 Sets of 6RM	3 Sets of 6RM
1 Set of 10RM	2 Sets of 10RM	3 Sets of 10RM

Table 4–3 Hypothetical Pattern of Progression in the Bench Press Exercise Using the Berger Training Program

Week	Monday	Wednesday	Friday
1	100 lbs × 6	100 lbs × 6	100 lbs × 6
	100 lbs × 5	100 lbs × 6	100 lbs × 6
	100 lbs × 4	100 lbs × 4	100 lbs × 6
2	105 lbs × 6	105 lbs × 6	105 lbs × 6
	105 lbs × 4	105 lbs × 5	105 lbs × 5
	105 lbs × 3	105 lbs × 4	105 lbs × 4
3	105 lbs × 6	105 lbs × 6	105 lbs × 6
	105 lbs × 6	105 lbs × 6	105 lbs × 6
	105 lbs × 5	105 lbs × 5	105 lbs × 6
4	110 lbs × 5	110 lbs × 5	110 lbs × 6
	110 lbs × 4	110 lbs × 4	110 lbs × 4
	110 lbs × 3	110 lbs × 4	110 lbs × 4
5	110 lbs × 6	110 lbs × 6	110 lbs × 6
	110 lbs × 5	110 lbs × 6	110 lbs × 5
	110 lbs × 5	110 lbs × 5	110 lbs × 5
6	110 lbs × 6	110 lbs × 6	115 lbs × 6
	110 lbs × 6	110 lbs × 6	115 lbs × 5
	110 lbs × 5	110 lbs × 6	115 lbs × 4

In contrast to the single training stimulus provided by the final set in the DeLorme-Watkins system, Berger's program calls for maximum effort on all three sets, because each set of six repetitions is done with the 6RM weightload. Nevertheless, the advantage of performing more than one set at maximum effort has never been clearly established. It is interesting to note that both Theodore Hettinger, the physician who conducted numerous experiments on isometric strength training during the early 1960s, and Ellington Darden, Director of Research for Nautilus Sports/Medical Industries, believe that one set per exercise at maximum effort is sufficient training stimulus to promote optimum strength development.

The Pyramid Program

In 1979, Westcott compared the training effects of the DeLorme-Watkins system and the Berger system, along with a third program that involved three sets with increasing weightloads and decreasing repetitions. The latter is a type of program commonly referred to as a pyramid system of training, because each set is done with more weight and fewer repetitions. Westcott's pyramid program was based on the exerciser's 1RM weightload, that is, the heaviest weightload he or she could lift once. The first set consisted of ten repetitions with 55 percent of the 1RM weightload, the second set required five repetitions with 75 percent of the 1RM weightload, and the third set was a single lift with 95 percent of the 1RM weightload.

Example

The heaviest weightload that Susan can bench press once (1RM weightload) is 100 pounds. According to Westcott's training formula, Susan should perform the following workout:

First Set: 10 repetitions with 55 pounds (55% 1RM weightload)
Second Set: 5 repetitions with 75 pounds (75% 1RM weightload)
Third Set: 1 repetition with 95 pounds (95% 1RM weightload)

The pyramid program is similar to the DeLorme-Watkins program in that both involve two progressively heavier warm-up sets, and one set designed to produce the training effect. They are different with respect to the relative amount of resistance used for the training stimulus in the final set. The DeLorme-Watkins program requires maximum effort (ten repetitions) with a submaximum resistance (10RM weightload). The pyramid program requires near-maximum effort (one repetition) with a near-maximum resistance (95% 1RM weightload).

Program Comparison

All of the participants in Westcott's study gained muscular strength, and the rates of strength development for the three training groups were quite similar. Results of the comparisons of the Berger system, the DeLorme-Watkins system, and the pyramid program are summarized in Table 4-4.

While the differences in the rates of strength improvement were not statistically significant, it is interesting to note two apparent trends with regard to these training programs. First, the training systems that required only one strenuous set (DeLorme-Watkins program and pyramid program) seemed to be more effective than the system that incorpo-

Table 4–4 Summary of Strength Gains Obtained with the DeLorme-Watkins, Berger, and Pyramid Training Programs

Training Group	Training Program	Mean Percent Strength Improvement per Week
Berger	6 × 6RM 6 × 6RM 6 × 6RM	3.7
DeLorme-Watkins	10 × 50% 10RM 10 × 75% 10RM 10 × 100% 10RM	4.3
Pyramid	10 × 55% 1RM 5 × 75% 1RM 1 × 95% 1RM	4.3

rated three strenuous sets (Berger program). Second, the training system based on the 1RM weightload (pyramid program) and the training system based on the 10RM weightload (DeLorme-Watkins program) appeared to be equally effective for increasing muscular strength.

The DeLorme-Watkins program requires a total of 30 repetitions, the Berger system a total of 18 repetitions, and the pyramid program a total of 16 repetitions. Yet, the results of Westcott's study indicate that the total number of repetitions may be a secondary consideration in terms of strength development. The more important factor seems to be the use of a relatively heavy resistance and a near-maximum muscular effort. One repetition with 95 percent of the 1RM weightload (pyramid program), six repetitions with the 6RM weightload (Berger system), and ten repetitions with the 10RM weightload (DeLorme-Watkins program) all require near-maximum muscular effort, and therefore produce a positive training effect. As demonstrated by Berger's (1965) study, it is not advisable to train with less than two-thirds of the 1RM weightload if one is interested in strength development, regardless of the number of repetitions performed.

Training Recommendations

It is suggested that a personal strength training program for free weights or Universal Gym equipment be designed in the following manner: For the final set of the training sequence, the exerciser should select a weightload between the 1RM and 10RM weightload, and execute as many repetitions as possible. The set prior to this should be performed with less resistance, and should be terminated before the point of acute muscle fatigue. The set before this should be the initial set of the workout. It should be done with even less resistance and should not approach the point of muscle fatigue.

Example

John prefers to do two repetitions with his 2RM weightload (140 pounds) for his final set of bench presses. He might therefore design his workout in the following manner:

First Set: 10 repetitions with 70 pounds
Second Set: 6 repetitions with 105 pounds
Third Set: 2 repetitions with 140 pounds

A program such as this would provide John with a warm-up set, a second set requiring moderate muscular effort, and a final set requiring maximum muscular effort.

Example

Karen chooses to execute eight repetitions with her 8RM weightload (50 pounds) for her final set of press-downs. She might, therefore, perform the following training sequence:

First Set: 8 repetitions with 30 pounds
Second Set: 8 repetitions with 40 pounds
Third Set: 8 repetitions with 50 pounds

This training program, although somewhat different from John's, also provides a warm-up set, a second set requiring moderate muscular effort, and a final set demanding maximum muscular effort. The basic pattern of a warm-up set, a set requiring moderate effort, and a set requiring maximum effort seems to be a key factor in progressive strength development, as long as the final set utilizes a relatively heavy resistance (10RM weightload or heavier). When a training program of this type is followed, the total number of repetitions performed during the training session does not appear to be an important factor.

SETS

The majority of strength training studies have utilized an exercise program consisting of three sets, with a predetermined number of repetitions per set. While research indicates that strength can be effectively increased under such a program, it is obvious that not everyone performs three sets with each exercise. Most persons who train on Nautilus equipment do only one set of 8 to 12 repetitions per exercise. Conversely, bodybuilders who train with conventional equipment (barbells and dumbbells) typically execute five to ten sets of 10 to 15 repetitions each with a variety of exercises. Olympic lifters and powerlifters, on the other hand, frequently execute five to ten sets of 1 to 5 repetitions each.

Bodybuilders

There are reasons for these differences in training approaches. Bodybuilders are more concerned with muscle appearance (size, shape, definition, proportion) than with muscle strength. This is not to say that bodybuilders are weak, only that their training objectives and training procedures reflect this particular emphasis. While there is very little scientific research on bodybuilding techniques, most physique contestants perform numerous sets and repetitions for every muscle group. The general consensus among bodybuilders is that muscle growth is most effectively stimulated by frequently saturating the muscle tissues with blood. This is referred to as a muscle "pump" and is achieved by executing several sets with high repetitions and little rest between sets.

Bodybuilders also favor this type of training because it is very vigorous and therefore consumes large amounts of energy. This is a major concern of most physique contestants because they do not want to appear "smooth" due to a fat layer between the muscles and the skin. They believe that performing many sets and repetitions helps burn up excess fat and results in better muscle definition, which they call muscle cuts.

They work particularly hard on this aspect of their training prior to a contest in order to show their muscles to the best possible advantage.

Olympic Lifters and Powerlifters

Olympic lifters and powerlifters are more concerned with muscle function than with muscle appearance. Their goal is to lift as much weight as possible in each of their competitive events. Although many Olympic and powerlifters have excellent, well-muscled physiques, they are less likely to train for muscle size, shape, definition, and proportion. Rather, their training focuses on increasing their muscular strength and improving their lifting technique. As indicated earlier in this chapter, the key to strength development is near-maximum training resistance. For this reason, competitive weightlifters train with relatively heavy weights, usually performing several sets of few repetitions each.

Another important aspect of competitive weightlifting is proper technique. Research clearly demonstrates that one can lift considerably more weight using biomechanically correct lifting techniques. There is, therefore, a great emphasis on lifting form and timing, particularly among the Olympic weightlifters. Because the neuromuscular patterns involved in lifting relatively light weights differ from those involved in lifting relatively heavy weights, most competitive weightlifters prefer to train with near-maximum resistance. In other words, they perform several sets of one or two repetitions each with near-maximum weightloads to perfect the form they will use when attempting maximum poundage under competitive conditions.

Unlike bodybuilders, competitive weightlifters typically rest for several minutes between sets. They must give their muscles ample time to recover from one set before attempting the next set in order to handle near-maximum weightloads and to complete their lifts with good form. Their routines also differ from those of bodybuilders in that fewer exercises are included. Competitive weightlifters generally practice their competition lifts (two for Olympic lifters, three for powerlifters) and a few supplemental exercises, rather than several exercises for the individual muscle groups.

Although competitive bodybuilders and competitive weightlifters train differently with regard to weightloads, repetitions, and rest periods, they are similar in that both groups tend to perform several sets with each exercise. While numerous sets may be necessary to achieve their particular training objectives, research indicates that fewer sets may be just as effective for the purpose of improving muscular strength.

A study by Redding (1971) did not reveal any strength-related differences between a training program utilizing two sets of five repetitions each and a training program incorporating five sets of two repetitions each. Another study of sets and repetitions (Kurtz 1968) compared Berger's training system with two popular strength programs, one that used eight sets per exercise and one that used ten sets per exercise. The results were divided, with the Berger system producing strength gains equivalent to the eight-set program, but not as great as the ten-set system. Whether one has the time or inclination to execute ten sets with every exercise in the training program is a question that only the exerciser can answer.

Training Recommendations

Most persons can achieve excellent, perhaps optimum, strength gains from a training program of three or fewer sets per exercise, as long as at least one set involves near-maximum resistance and near-maximum muscular effort. Proponents of Nautilus training advocate only one set of 8 to 12 repetitions for each exercise. They contend that a single exercise bout to the point of muscle failure is the best possible stimulus for strength development, and there is little evidence to contradict their claim. It is recalled from Westcott's (1974) study on training frequency (see Chapter Three) that executing more sets per exercise requires more recovery time between training sessions. Therefore, persons who prefer to perform several sets of each exercise must be careful to provide sufficient recovery time between workouts to enable positive strength adaptations to occur.

For persons who train with conventional weights or Universal Gym equipment, the three set program described earlier in this chapter is recommended. This pattern of doing a warm-up set, a set requiring moderate effort, and a set requiring maximum effort seems to be a safe, effective, and enjoyable method of strength development.

REST INTERVALS

The Principle of Rebuilding Time (see Chapter Three) states that after a muscle is stressed beyond its normal demands, a certain amount of time is needed for the tissues to recover and make positive physiological adaptations. If the rest interval between successive training sessions is too brief, the muscle will not be able to rebuild to a higher level of strength before being stressed again. Conversely, if the rest interval following a workout is too long, the resultant strength gains will not be maintained and the muscle will gradually return to its previous strength level.

It is important, therefore, to determine either the optimal rest period for a given training program, or the optimal training program for a given rest period. That is, if one has a particular training program of exercises, sets, and repetitions, one should experiment with a longer or shorter recovery interval and note the effect on strength development. Quite possibly, changing from an every other day training schedule to an every third day training schedule may increase one's rate of strength gain. On the other hand, there are those who seem to thrive on a four sessions per week or five sessions per week training frequency.

Perhaps it is more practical to first arrange one's workout schedule and then adjust one's training routine accordingly. For example, if the only opportunities college students have to visit the weightroom are Monday, Wednesday, and Friday afternoons, then they should experiment with the intensity of the training program. They may discover that training harder increases the rate of strength development, or that cutting down the workout actually produces better results.

It is recalled that Westcott (1974) found a direct relationship between the length of the training session and the duration of the recovery period. (See Chapter Three, Principle of Rebuilding Time.) In other words, the more sets executed during the workout, the longer one should rest between successive training sessions. Westcott's study indicated that the strength of the bench press muscles (chest, shoulders, triceps) can be increased at a rate of about 3 percent per week when the workout-recovery relation is appropriate, even though the number of sets performed during each workout varies widely.

Significance of the Recovery Interval

The significance of the recovery period between workout sessions is undoubtedly the most misunderstood factor in strength development. After all, it is the quantity and the quality of the rest interval that is responsible for the repair and growth of the muscle tissues. The basic function of the training session is to stress and fatigue muscle tissues, whereas the basic function of the recovery period is to allow these tissues time to rebuild to a higher level of strength. Consequently, muscular development is influenced as much by how one rests as by how one exercises, and neither is beneficial without the other.

An almost universal mistake of both novice and advanced weight trainers is to increase the intensity of their training sessions without making a corresponding adjustment in their recovery procedures. This results in reduced muscular gains and eventually leads to a strength plateau. Unfortunately, most persons respond to a strength plateau by training harder in an attempt to force muscle development. As previously indicated, however, the only thing that intensified training can accomplish at this point is greater muscle fatigue. This maintains the strength plateau, and eventually results in loss of strength. Perhaps the most difficult lesson for most strength enthusiasts to learn is that muscle growth occurs between training sessions. Training hard is only one aspect of strength development. The positive physiological adaptations actually take place during the non-training interval. Many persons never understand this vital concept and give up in despair, exclaiming that "I'm training twice as hard as I used to but I'm not getting any stronger."

Another common mistake among competitive weightlifters is to train harder than usual a week or two before a contest. Almost invariably, those who increase their training intensity prior to a contest perform more poorly than anticipated, whereas those who decrease their training intensity prior to a contest perform better than expected. It is important to realize that muscles rapidly become weaker (fatigued) during the training session, and gradually become stronger during the recovery period.

Another point sometimes hard to understand is that the advanced exerciser needs more rest than the novice. Remember that the length of the rest period is proportional to the length of the training session. Because a relatively short workout is enough to fatigue the untrained muscles of a beginner, a relatively short recovery period is sufficient for positive strength adaptations to occur. On the other hand, seasoned weight trainers need a more strenuous workout to adequately stress their well-conditioned muscles, and this requires a correspondingly longer rest period. While the beginner may initially gain strength by taking four or five hard workouts a week, the more advanced exerciser will usually make better progress with two or three hard training sessions per week.

Recommended Rest Period

Due to the fact that every individual responds differently to muscular stress, it is not possible to suggest a specific number of hours or days that one should rest between workouts. This would be as unwise as insisting that everyone take exactly seven hours of sleep each night. Some people simply need more sleep than others, and some athletes likewise require more recovery time than others. The best means of determining one's optimal rest period is to keep an accurate record of one's training results, as well as comments regarding one's subjective feelings during each workout. This is more easily accomplished by means of a workout logbook such as that presented in Figure 4–2. Note that both objective data and subjective feelings are included in the sample training log to help the exerciser make better judgments regarding his or her training program. The time required to complete a workout logbook is a small investment that is likely to pay large dividends in progressive strength gains with a minimum of injuries and setbacks. Let the logbook be your guide. If strength development stops (plateaus), it would be prudent to decrease the length of the workout, increase the length of the recovery period, or both. Likewise, persistent feelings of weakness, tiredness, or lack of enthusiasm are symptoms of insufficient rest and should be treated accordingly. Carefully monitored trial and error procedures can be an effective means for establishing and re-establishing a training program that produces optimum strength development.

As a guideline, if the muscles are too weak to complete a second workout after a one day rest, it would indicate that a longer recovery period is necessary. If the exerciser finds that two days after a particular workout, he or she is able to perform the same workout with less effort, this would suggest that a two-day recovery period is appropriate. If, after a three-day recovery period, the exerciser feels rested but has just as much difficulty executing the latter training session, it would be logical to assume that too much rest had been taken between workouts.

RECOMMENDED REST INTERVAL BETWEEN SETS

The length of the rest intervals between sets during a given workout is another important training consideration. Basically, the amount of

Workout Logbook

Date: _____ Start: _____ Finish: _____ Time:_____

Exercise: _____   Exercise: _____

Set:	1	2	3
Reps:	____	____	____
Wtld:	____	____	____
Rest Btwn Sets:	____	____	____

Set:	1	2	3
Reps:	____	____	____
Wtld:	____	____	____
Rest Btwn Sets:	____	____	____

Exercise: _____   Exercise: _____

Set:	1	2	3
Reps:	____	____	____
Wtld:	____	____	____
Rest Btwn Sets:	____	____	____

Set:	1	2	3
Reps:	____	____	____
Wtld:	____	____	____
Rest Btwn Sets:	____	____	____

Exercise: _____   Exercise: _____

Set:	1	2	3
Reps:	____	____	____
Wtld:	____	____	____
Rest Btwn Sets:	____	____	____

Set:	1	2	3
Reps:	____	____	____
Wtld:	____	____	____
Rest Btwn Sets:	____	____	____

Rest Since Last Workout: _____

Bodyweight: _____

Measurements: _____

Feelings:			
	Strong	Average	Weak
	Energetic	Average	Tired
	Fast	Average	Slow
	Enthusiastic	Average	Unenthusiastic

Figure 4–2 Sample workout logbook with attention to both objective data and subjective feelings.

rest people take between sets is dependent upon their training objectives. As indicated earlier in the chapter, competitive bodybuilders typically take very brief rests between successive bouts of exercise. They believe that a short rest period enables them to achieve a better muscle pump. That is, exercise sets performed in quick succession result in a greater saturation of the muscle tissues with blood. Bodybuilders spend most of their workout time in vigorous activity in order to develop muscle definition.

Competitive weightlifters, on the other hand, tend to rest several minutes after each set of exercises, because their primary training objective is to lift heavier barbells. Because they train with near-maximum weightloads, a lengthy recovery period is necessary for their muscles to be as fresh as possible for each new lift. They feel that this is the best way to train for increased strength and improved technique.

Most persons who train with weights would do well to take a little more rest than competitive bodybuilders and a little less rest than competitive weightlifters. Although the process of acute muscle fatigue is not clearly understood, probably most exercisers have pushed their muscles to the point of momentary failure and experienced the accompanying discomfort. Momentary failure appears to accurately describe the phenomenon in which one minute the muscle can no longer move the weightload, and the next minute is capable of completing several repetitions with the same resistance.

One factor at least partly responsible for acute muscle fatigue is the depletion of the primary source of energy that enables the muscle to contract against relatively heavy resistance. This energy source, composed of adenosine triphosphate and phosphocreatine, is referred to as *phosphagen.* Phosphagen stores provide large amounts of energy for short periods of time. For example, a ten-second bout of near-maximum work would essentially deplete a muscle's available phosphagen stores. Fortunately, phosphagens are quickly replenished. Within about 30 seconds 50 percent of the phosphagen stores are refilled. After another 30 seconds an additional 25 percent of the phosphagen stores are ready for action. Thirty seconds later another 12.5 percent of the phosphagens are available, and so on. Table 4–5 provides further information on the rate of phosphagen replenishment during the rest period following an all-out bout of exercises.

As seen in Table 4–5, the phosphagen stores are largely replenished

Table 4–5   Approximate Replenishment Process of Phosphagen Energy Stores

Approximate Time Elapsed since Depletion of Phosphagen Stores	Approximate Percentage of Phosphagen Stores Replenished
0 seconds	0.00
30 seconds	50.00
60 seconds (1 minute)	75.00
90 seconds	87.50
120 seconds (2 minutes)	93.75
150 seconds	96.88
180 seconds (3 minutes)	98.44
210 seconds	99.22
240 seconds (4 minutes)	99.61
270 seconds	99.80
300 seconds (5 minutes)	99.90

within two minutes following a strenuous exercise bout, such as ten repetitions with the 10RM weightload. It should be noted that rest intervals of less than one minute do not permit adequate phosphagen restoration for performance at maximum capacity. Also, rest intervals greater than three minutes do not increase phosphagen supplies significantly, since the stores are almost completely (98.44 percent) replenished by this time.

Although energy restoration is only one aspect of muscle fatigue, rest intervals of about two minutes are appropriate for most training purposes. Those persons particularly interested in obtaining a muscle "pump" could cut down to a minute rest interval or less, and those persons primarily concerned with handling near-maximum poundages could lengthen their rest period to three minutes or more. A partial recovery (one minute or less) seems to facilitate muscle hypertrophy by keeping a large quantity of blood congested in the muscles, whereas a full recovery (three minutes or more) appears best suited for increasing muscle strength, because the exerciser is able to use heavier weightloads.

When performing only one set per exercise, or when completing a circuit of exercises, the rest interval can be cut down considerably, as long as successive exercises do not stress the same major muscle groups. For example, if one were to perform a set of squats (thighs), a set of bench presses (chest), a set of lat bar pull-downs (back), a set of triceps press-downs (triceps), a set of curls (biceps), and a set of upright rows (shoulders), it would not be necessary to take more than a few seconds rest between sets, because each exercise utilizes a different prime mover muscle group.

SUMMARY OF KEY TRAINING VARIABLES

The training procedures one follows should be specific to the training objectives one wants to achieve. Although any well-designed training program should result in both strength gains and muscle hypertrophy, optimal attainment in either area is dependent upon specialized training procedures. Basically, a strength oriented program involves fewer exercises, heavier weightloads, fewer sets, fewer repetitions, and longer recovery intervals than a size-oriented program does. Although the physiological responses are not clearly understood, it appears that the key to strength development is relatively heavy weightloads, whereas the key to muscle hypertrophy is relatively short recovery periods between successive sets of exercise. Table 4–6 summarizes the most important training variables and the recommended training practices for achieving greater muscle strength and greater muscle size.

Table 4–6 Summary of Key Training Variables

	Strength	*Size*
Exercises	1 per muscle group	2–4 per muscle group
Weightload	80–90% 1RM	70–80% 1RM
Sets	2–4 sets per exercise	4–6 sets per exercise
Repetitions	2–6 repetitions per set	8–12 repetitions per set
Rest between Sets	3 minute minimum	1 minute maximum

SAMPLE TRAINING PROGRAMS

The following sample training programs are based on the information in the preceding section. Table 4–7 is a sample training session for the person interested in developing muscle strength. It consists of one exercise for each major muscle group (excluding lower legs and forearms), variations of the 10RM weightload, and a three-minute recovery period between sets. The total time requirement for this workout is about 70 minutes.

Table 4–8 is a sample workout for the person who desires greater muscle size (hypertrophy). It consists of two exercises for each major muscle group (excluding lower legs and forearms), performed consecutively with only one-minute recovery between sets to promote the muscle pumping phenomenon. This procedure increases the level of muscle

Table 4–7 Sample Training Session Designed for Increased Muscle Strength

Exercise	Muscle Group	Wt Ld*	Set#1	Rest	Set#2	Rest	Set#3	Total Time
Bench Press	Chest	10RM	10 rep	3 min	10 rep	3 min	10 rep	9 min
Lat Pull-down	Back	10RM	10 rep	3 min	10 rep	3 min	10 rep	9 min
Upright Row	Shoulder	10RM	10 rep	3 min	10 rep	3 min	10 rep	9 min
Triceps Press-down	Tricep	10RM	10 rep	3 min	10 rep	3 min	10 rep	9 min
Biceps Curl	Bicep	10RM	10 rep	3 min	10 rep	3 min	10 rep	9 min
Leg Extension	Quadricep	10RM	10 rep	3 min	10 rep	3 min	10 rep	9 min
Leg Curl	Hamstring	10RM	10 rep	3 min	10 rep	3 min	10 rep	9 min
Trunk Curl	Abdominal	10RM	10 rep	3 min	10 rep	3 min	10 rep	9 min

Total Repetitions = 240
Total Time = 72 minutes

* The first set is executed with 60 percent of the 10RM weightload, the second set is performed with 80 percent of the 10RM weightload, and the third set is completed with the 10RM weightload.

fatigue and reduces the number of repetitions that can be completed on the second and third sets of the exercise. The total time requirement for this workout is also 70 minutes.

Table 4–8 Sample Training Session Designed for Increased Muscle Size (Hypertrophy)

Exercise	Muscle Group	Wt Ld*	Set#1	Rest	Set#2	Rest	Set#3	Total Time
Bench Press	Chest	10RM	10 rep	1 min	10 rep	1 min	10 rep	5 min
DB Flies	Chest	10RM	10 rep	1 min	10 rep	1 min	10 rep	5 min
Lat Pull-down	Back	10RM	10 rep	1 min	10 rep	1 min	10 rep	5 min
DB Bent Row	Back	10RM	10 rep	1 min	10 rep	1 min	10 rep	5 min
Upright Row	Shoulder	10RM	10 rep	1 min	10 rep	1 min	10 rep	5 min
Alt DB Press	Shoulder	10RM	10 rep	1 min	10 rep	1 min	10 rep	5 min
Triceps Press-down	Tricep	10RM	10 rep	1 min	10 rep	1 min	10 rep	5 min
DB Triceps Extension	Tricep	10RM	10 rep	1 min	10 rep	1 min	10 rep	5 min
Biceps Curl	Bicep	10RM	10 rep	1 min	10 rep	1 min	10 rep	5 min
Seated Curl	Bicep	10RM	10 rep	1 min	10 rep	1 min	10 rep	5 min
Half Squat	Quads/Hams	10RM	10 rep	1 min	10 rep	1 min	10 rep	5 min
DB Jump Squat	Quads/Hams	10RM	10 rep	1 min	10 rep	1 min	10 rep	5 min
Trunk Curl	Abdominals	10 lbs	30 rep	1 min	30 rep	1 min	30 rep	5 min
Incline Situp	Midsection	10 lbs	15 rep	1 min	15 rep	1 min	15 rep	5 min

Total Repetitions = 495
Total Time = 70 Minutes

* All three sets are performed with the 10RM weightload.

Chapter Five

Training Considerations

TRAINING FREQUENCY

Most strength authorities recommend a three day per week strength training schedule. Although any three non-consecutive days are acceptable, most persons adhere to a Monday-Wednesday-Friday program with no strength-related activities on Tuesday, Thursday, Saturday, or Sunday. Such a program has many benefits, both physiological and psychological. Even competitive bodybuilders who train for several hours daily seldom perform the same exercises during successive workouts, thereby providing individual muscle groups with a two-day recovery period.

While the alternate-day training program is very popular among weight trainers, some people do question the need for a 48-hour recovery period between workouts. They point out that many athletes and laborers perform vigorous physical activity day after day without any apparent problems. For example, runners, swimmers, gymnasts, wrestlers, cyclists, lumberjacks, longshoremen, and construction workers stress the same muscle groups every day and still seem to obtain desirable training effects. What is it about weight training that makes a two-day rest between training sessions necessary?

The answer to this question is directly related to the dual characteristics of a successful strength training program, *muscle isolation* and *stress intensification.* The well-designed strength training program exemplifies muscle isolation and stress intensification in a way that few other activities can duplicate. The principal reason for a variety of weight training exercises is that each exercise uses as few muscle groups as possible. Bodybuilding magazines are replete with specific exercises for individual muscle groups.

In most physical activities, including those previously listed, several muscle groups work together, sharing the stress of the exercise and the effects of fatigue. Persons who train with weights, on the other hand, go to great lengths to isolate specific muscle groups so that one or two muscles bear the entire brunt of the exercise. Take, for example, barbell curls, an exercise that primarily affects the biceps muscles. Most gyms pride themselves on having curling benches that support the upper arms to eliminate all assisting movements from other muscle groups during biceps curls. It does not take many curls on the "Scott" bench or "preacher" bench to thoroughly exhaust the biceps muscles, something that is seldom experienced outside the weightroom.

Once a particular muscle group is effectively isolated, other muscles are unable to compensate for an increase in stress, as happens under ordinary circumstances. When performing regular barbell curls, for example, stress intensification often results in compensatory movements such as bending at the waist, swinging the barbell, hyperextending the back, and using momentum to a greater degree than muscle strength. However, when executing barbell curls on a curling bench, stress intensification must be met squarely by the biceps muscles themselves. Under these conditions an increase in stress means an increase in the contractile force required of the biceps up to the point of muscle failure.

Because weight training equipment makes possible both muscle isolation and stress intensification, individual muscle groups can be subjected to far greater stress than they normally experience in other types of athletic training or physical work. It therefore makes sense to rest for 48 hours between stressful weight training sessions.

However, depending upon one's training program, a recovery period of more than or less than 48 hours may produce better results. Research indicates that comparable gains in strength can be achieved from various frequencies of weight training. Several studies on this aspect of strength training have demonstrated similar increases in muscular strength from programs incorporating one, two, three, and five training sessions per week.

In one such study, Westcott (1974) divided a weekly bench press workout of 60 repetitions with near-maximum resistance into one, two, three, and five training sessions. Group 1-a-week performed all 60 repetitions on Monday and rested the other six days. Subjects in this group executed 12 sets of 5 repetitions with the 5RM weightload. Group 2-a-week performed 30 repetitions on Monday and 30 repetitions on Friday. Subjects in this group executed 6 sets of 5 repetitions with the 5RM weightload during each training session. Group 3-a-week did 20 repetitions every Monday, Wednesday, and Friday. These subjects completed 4 sets of 5 repetitions with the 5RM weightload during each training session. Group 5-a-week performed 12 repetitions every day, Monday through Friday. These subjects executed 2 sets of 6 repetitions with the 6RM weightload during each training session. The training programs for the four experimental groups are summarized in Table 5–1.

The results of Westcott's study revealed that all four groups increased strength at the rate of about 2 to 3 percent per week. Although analyses of the data did not reveal any statistically significant differences among the four training programs in terms of strength improvement, a trend was apparent. As shown in Figure 5–1, the groups that trained more frequently with fewer sets seemed to experience faster rates of strength gain than the groups that trained less often with more sets.

Table 5–1 Summary of Training Programs and Results in Westcott's Study of Training Frequency

Group	Workout Program	Training Frequency	Repetitions per Week	Avg. Strength Gain (%/week)
Five-a-week (n = 6)	2 sets × 6 reps (12 reps)	5 sessions/wk (M T W R F)	60	2.9
Three-a-week (n = 13)	4 sets × 5 reps (20 reps)	3 sessions/wk (M W F)	60	3.1
Two-a-week (n = 20)	6 sets × 5 reps (30 reps)	2 sessions/wk (M F)	60	2.2
One-a-week (n = 16)	12 sets × 5 reps (60 reps)	1 session/wk (M)	60	2.6

When corrected for the size of the groups, the mean strength gain for Group 1-a-week and Group 2-a-week was 2.38 percent per week, whereas the mean strength gain for Group 3-a-week and Group 5-a-week was 3.04 percent per week.

Recommendation

Relatively long and infrequent workouts may be somewhat less effective than relatively short and frequent training sessions for promoting strength development. Neither long and frequent workouts nor short and infrequent workouts are advisable. The former training pattern leads to chronic muscle fatigue, and the latter training program fails to provide sufficient training stimuli to promote positive muscle adaptations. When following the guidelines for weightloads, sets, repetitions, and rest periods recommended in this chapter, a training frequency of three days per week is advisable. If a more vigorous training program is desired,

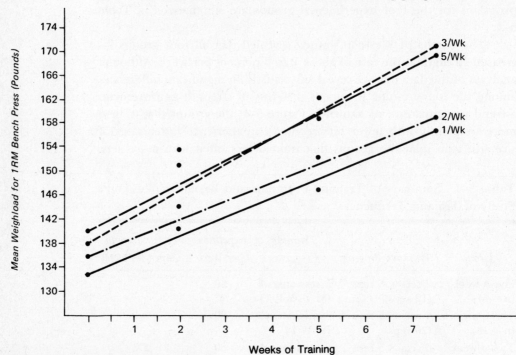

Figure 5–1 Mean improvement in the 1RM bench press over a 7½ week period for groups training one, two, three, and five times per week.

the training frequency should be decreased. Conversely, if one prefers to train more often, the workout should be made less arduous so that the exerciser can be physically and psychologically ready for each new training session.

TRAINING TIME

The actual training time necessary to complete a given program is almost always less than the amount of time the exerciser spends in the weightroom. As with any other athletic activity, strength training is a social phenomenon, and one of the reasons people frequent the weightroom is to talk with other strength enthusiasts. Unlike runners, who are able to talk to each other during their runs, weight trainers cannot talk while they are exercising.

There are basically three times when communications among weight trainers can occur; before beginning the workout, during the rest intervals, and after finishing the workout. While weight trainers are encouraged to talk with each other before and after their workouts, they should not normally engage in conversation other than encouragement during the recovery periods between sets of exercises. Unless one is highly disciplined, it is too easy to keep talking instead of starting the next exercise bout on schedule. These delays and extended rest periods reduce the training stimulus, and drag the workout into a long and less productive ordeal.

Weight training sessions should be characterized by a relatively high percentage of activity time. Because the activity is so intensely strenuous, there must be some recovery time between successive exercise bouts. However, rest periods of more than three minutes are generally not necessary, and may very well be counterproductive. Consider the following example.

Example

John trains six days per week. On Monday, Wednesday, and Friday he performs five exercises (one each for the chest, shoulders, back, triceps, and biceps), and on Tuesday, Thursday, and Saturday he performs five different exercises (one each for the abdominals, quadriceps, hamstrings, lower legs, and forearms). His training program consists of three sets of ten repetitions for each exercise. If each set of ten repetitions takes about 45 seconds to complete, and if John rests 2 minutes between sets, the total workout time necessary to complete three sets of five exercises is about 40 minutes. Of this, the actual training time is about 12 minutes and the total resting time is about 28 minutes. In other words, John's workout is approximately 30 percent activity time and 70 percent resting time.

A 40-minute workout in which 15 sets of exercises are completed is, by most standards, a very efficient training session. Many persons take up to three times as long to finish a comparable workout. While there is nothing wrong with spending an hour and a half in the training facility, the workout itself should be relatively brief and intense. Time spent in talking, stretching, warming-up, and cooling-down should precede and follow the weight workout, but should not generally be a part of it.

Time of Day

Another aspect of training time is that part of the day when one exercises. Research indicates that the time of day one trains does not significantly affect the training progress. When one trains appears to be basically a matter of personal preference. Some people like to train in the morning when they are rested and their muscles feel fresh. Others prefer to train later in the day when they are fully awake and their muscles feel loose. Some persons even schedule their training session just before bedtime. The only time strenuous exercise of any kind is definitely to be avoided is immediately following a large meal. Because strenuous exercise diverts blood flow from the digestive organs to the active muscles, the digestive process is delayed, food remains in the stomach longer, and discomfort is likely to be experienced as the exercise continues. For this reason, vigorous weight training should not be attempted within one to two hours after a large meal. Other than this rather obvious exception, there is no evidence that any time of day is more or less advantageous for engaging in strength training activities and obtaining desirable training effects.

There is some debate as to whether people should consistently train at the same time of day or purposely vary their training schedule. One leading strength authority believes that once the body grows accustomed to a particular pattern of training it is more difficult to stimulate strength gains. Others feel that regularity is an important aspect of a successful strength training program.

It may be that different types of people respond differently to regimented training schedules. Persons who characteristically follow a regular pattern of daily activities are likely to make better progress on a relatively fixed training schedule. On the other hand, persons who enjoy variety and avoid schedules whenever possible are advised to frequently change their workout time. These persons are also encouraged to experiment with different combinations of sets, repetitions, and rest periods, since they seem to respond more favorably to diversified training stimuli.

As with many other aspects of strength training, the guidelines for determining the various components associated with training time are only a starting point. You are urged to experiment with the training variables to discover which procedures work best for you.

TRAINING PARTNERS

Training partners are an asset to one's strength training progress. Regardless of the training program, exercise facilities, or equipment employed, a training partner fulfills a definite role. The most important thing a training partner can do is encourage the exerciser throughout the workout, and particularly during the final repetitions of each exercise set. This does not mean idle talking during the rest intervals, but genuine encouragement prior to and during each exercise bout. The solo exerciser hears only one voice, that of his or her tired muscles saying "that's enough." Persons who train together hear a second voice, that of their partners urging them to squeeze out one more repetition.

Although some persons train with more drive and singleness of purpose than others, most persons admit that they work harder when they have a training partner. Actually, each partner inspires the other by alternately giving encouragement and exhibiting maximum effort during his or her own exercise bouts. This modeling effect is a significant advantage of partner training. Seeing one's partner go all-out on an exercise set, regardless of the weightload, is a great source of motivation. Outstanding coaches in all sports areas typically work their athletes in pairs or small groups for this very reason. One is less likely to merely go through the motions of a workout when a training partner is giving an unrestrained effort.

In addition to serving as a source of encouragement and motivation, training partners make a workout more interesting. After completing a set of exercises one uses the rest interval to watch, encourage, and assist the training partner, rather than to think about how tired one's own muscles feel. The workout progresses more quickly, with just enough time to make notations in the logbook before starting the next exercise bout.

Spotters

Depending on the type of exercise being performed, training partners may be absolutely necessary. It is foolish to attempt heavy bench presses without a spotter, because an unanticipated event, such as a muscle tear, muscle spasm, or muscle cramp, could result in serious injury. The same is true for squats, pull-overs, and any other exercise in which momentary loss of muscle control could have serious consequences.

In addition to safety considerations, the training partner can perform a valuable service in these and other exercises. For example, the exerciser may be unable to push the final repetition in the bench press past the halfway point. If the spotter gently supports a small percentage of the weightload instead of quickly lifting the bar to the standards, the exerciser will be able to force the bar upward and complete the repetition. This is referred to as a *forced repetition,* and is made possible by a competent training partner who gives just enough help to allow the lifter to complete the movement and more fully stress the contributing muscle groups. Forced repetitions are a standard training practice among most bodybuilders, since their goal is to continue each exercise bout to the point of maximum muscle exertion.

Along the same line, some exercisers include so-called negative work in their strength training program. It is recalled that negative work involves maximum effort against a resistance that is too great for the muscle to overcome. This is actually an eccentric contraction in which the muscle lengthens under the force of an overpowering resistance (weightload). For example, an individual may not be able to curl more than 90 pounds from the waist to the shoulders. However, the same person could *slowly* lower a 100-pound barbell from the shoulders to the waist by means of maximum eccentric muscle contraction. Many people believe that controlled failure (eccentric contraction) with 100 pounds provides a greater training stimulus than success (concentric contraction) with 90 pounds. For those who train in this manner, one or more partners are essential to bring the weightload to the desired starting position.

While there are several exercises in which a partner is helpful, there are others that simply cannot be done as effectively without the aid of a partner. Various stretching exercises, particularly those for the back and hamstrings are greatly enhanced by a knowledgeable person who gently holds the partner in a stretched position, and gradually extends the range of motion. Likewise, many isometric exercises, such as those for the neck muscles, depend on a skilled training partner who provides the right amount of resistance in the right place at the right time.

The advantage of training with one or more partners far outweighs any disadvantage, provided the partners are compatible and have similar training goals and procedures. It is not necessary for the partners to be equally matched in strength if training is done on Universal Gym or Nautilus equipment, since weightloads can be changed quickly and easily. However, if conventional weights are utilized, the partners should not be vastly different in terms of muscle strength or much of their workout time and energy will be used for changing the weights.

TRAINING SAFETY

Training safety is more than merely avoiding large-scale accidents. There are many aspects of safe training, including the prevention of sprains, strains, tears, and other soft tissue injuries. Basically, safe training procedures can be categorized into three general areas: 1) training equipment, 2) training space, and 3) training technique.

Training Equipment

All training apparatus should be in good working order and periodically checked for wear. Imagine what could happen if a bench press standard collapsed with a 250-pound barbell resting on it, or if the cable snapped during heavy lat bar pull-downs. Safe equipment implies snug fitting collars which stay in place and secure the weight plates on the barbells and dumbbells during exercises. It also means barbell sleeves that revolve smoothly, pulleys that spin without sticking points, and exercise machines that operate without difficulties.

Proper adjustment for the individual exerciser, particularly on complex apparatus such as Nautilus machines, is also important. These machines are carefully designed to accommodate individual differences, such as limb lengths, and should always be repositioned for each new exerciser. The time used in making such adjustments is time well spent, since it increases the muscle training effects and decreases the possibility of injury.

Training Space

Most weightroom accidents are the result of training space violations. Weight training requires much more space than most people realize. Ample space is obviously needed for free-weight exercises in which barbells and dumbbells are moving in every direction. Space is also needed around exercise machines, and people should give wide berth to machines that are in use. Moving pulleys, cams, cables, and weight-stacks can all cause serious injuries when someone steps too near or leans against a machine carelessly. Even calisthenics-type exercises such as situps, pull-ups, bar dips, and pushups require considerable amounts of space to be executed correctly.

Space is also necessary for movement among the various stations. Traffic lanes must be free from machines, weight plates, and other items, as well as persons who are exercising. This means that other space must be available for placing weight plates, barbells, dumbbells, training belts, cables, towels, etc. There must also be areas of sufficient size to accommodate persons who are lifting, stretching, warming up, cooling down, conversing, or writing in their logbooks. In other words, the safe strength training facility should be spacious and uncluttered. Exercise stations should not be close together and weight training equipment should not be left on the floor. Every item in the weightroom should have a particular place to be stored and specific places to be used. A neat and orderly strength training facility is absolutely essential for the safety of the exercisers.

Finally, space violations often result in injuries to spotters. When spotting an exercise, such as the bench press or squat, it is not necessary for the spotter to be right on top of the lifter. It is best to give the lifter plenty of room and to be ready to step in to give assistance if necessary. Even when the spotter is providing added resistance for negative work, he or she should find the most unobtrusive position to work from, and give the lifter as much room as possible to execute the exercise movements.

Training Techniques

Accidents frequently occur as a result of improper training techniques. Persons who throw weights are more likely to injure themselves than persons who use controlled movement speeds. Persons who perform unsupported exercises, such as the standing press, have a higher risk of injury than those who do supported exercises, such as the incline press. Figure 5–2 illustrates the greater stress to the lower back imposed by unsupported overhead pressing movements.

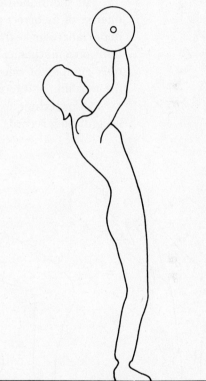

Supported
(Incline Bench Press)

Unsupported
(Standing Press)

Figure 5–2 Comparison of overhead pressing movements from a supported (incline bench press) position and an unsupported (standing press) position. Note the hyperextension of the lower back characteristic of the latter exercise.

Many muscle injuries result from ignorance of basic biomechanical principles. (See Chapter Three.) For example, due to leverage factors, much less weight must be used for straight arm exercises (e.g., straight arm flies, straight arm pull-overs) than for bent arm exercises (e.g., bent arm flies, bent arm pull-overs). Unfavorable leverage arrangements are also responsible for subjecting the lower back muscles to high stress conditions in exercises such as good mornings, bent rows, and stiff-legged dead lifts. (See Figure 5–3.)

As mentioned earlier, improper technique is an inevitable consequence of incorrect positioning on an exercise machine. It is therefore important to make the appropriate adjustments prior to executing repetitions on a mechanical exercise apparatus. For example, when using Nautilus equipment one should make certain that the axis of rotation on the machine is directly in line with the joint being exercised.

Poor technique is frequently exhibited during attempts at personal weightlifting records. The prospect of establishing a new personal record

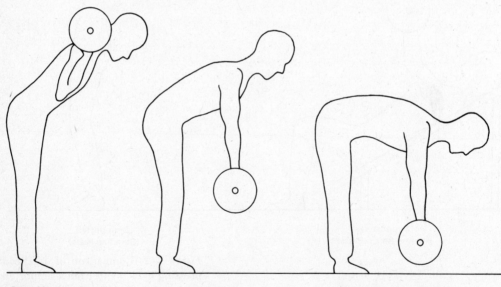

Good Morning Exercise   Bent Row   Stiff-Legged Dead Lift

Figure 5–3 Three exercises that subject the lower back musculature to high stress conditions due to unfavorable leverage factors.

is often sufficient incentive to cheat on a lift. Bridging on a bench press and arching on a standing curl are common maneuvers that permit heavier lifts, but place great stress on the lower back. (See Figure 5–4.) Perhaps the most necessary change in the field of weight training is to place greater emphasis on lifting a heavy weight correctly than on lifting a heavier weight incorrectly.

Due to the intensity of most weight training exercises, injuries tend to be relatively severe, and often require several weeks for rehabilitation. Because many people discontinue weight training altogether after experiencing a debilitating injury, it is important to be extra safety conscious in the weight training room. Frequent equipment checks, ample training space, and proper exercise techniques are the keys to injury-free and enjoyable weight training programs.

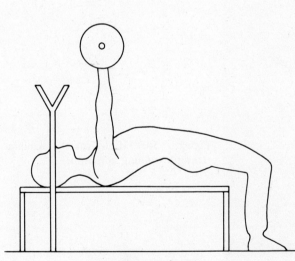

Bench Press with Bridge

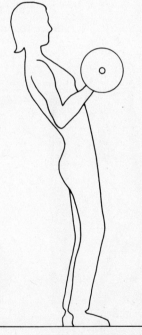

Curl with Back Bend

Figure 5–4 Incorrect form in the bench press exercise and standing curl exercise place great stress on the muscles of the lower back.

STRENGTH TRAINING EQUIPMENT

If money and training space were no object, a strength training enthusiast could choose from among at least five different types of training equipment, not including isometrics, springs, elastic cables, and similar training devices. The five types of strength training equipment in greatest use at the present time are: 1) Cybex isokinetic machines, 2) Mini-Gym isokinetic apparatus, 3) conventional barbells and dumbbells, 4) Universal Gym equipment, and 5) Nautilus Sports machines. Due to the fact that Cybex equipment is currently used primarily for strength testing, muscle rehabilitation, and research purposes, it will not be presented as a viable training alternative for the majority of strength enthusiasts.

Mini-Gym

Mini-Gym produces training devices that provide isokinetic resistance to a muscle movement. (See Figure 5–5.) Isokinetic training implies

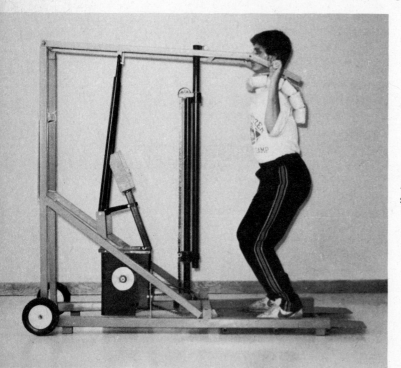

Figure 5–5 Mini-Gym isokinetic strength training apparatus.

that the resistance varies automatically in accordance with the applied muscular force. That is, if muscle force increases the resistance increases proportionately, and if muscle force decreases, the resistance decreases proportionately. To better understand how the isokinetic principle works, stand in the shallow end of a swimming pool and move your arm through the water. When you apply little force your arm meets little resistance from the water and moves slowly in the desired direction. When you apply greater force, your arm encounters greater resistance from the water and again moves slowly in the desired direction. Because the muscular force is always met by an almost equivalent amount of resistance, isokinetic exercises are characterized by relatively slow and steady movement speeds.

Mini-Gym training equipment provides isokinetic resistance by means of a hydraulic clutch which regulates movement speed through frictional forces. As greater muscle force is applied, greater frictional forces are produced, resulting in a proportionate increase in resistance and a steady movement speed. Although Mini-Gym equipment automatically accommodates the resistance to the applied force, it is useful only for concentric contractions (positive work). Eccentric contractions (negative work) cannot be performed with isokinetic equipment.

The relatively small size and the mobility of the basic Mini-Gym apparatus facilitates a wide variety of exercise uses. Almost any athletic skill can be simulated with Mini-Gym equipment, as can most exercises performed with conventional weight training equipment. See Appendix A for more information on Mini-Gym isokinetic strength training devices.

Barbells and Dumbbells

Barbells and dumbbells have been basic to strength training programs for years, and are still the most familiar and widely used type of exercise equipment. (See Figure 5–6.) Between barbells, designed for two-handed lifts, and dumbbells, designed for one-handed lifts, a number of exercises can be performed with free weights. As the name implies, free weights are not attached to any fixtures or machines, and can be manipulated by the exerciser in any way desired.

Free weights can be used for both concentric contractions (positive work) and eccentric contractions (negative work). However, because the muscles and bones of the body function as lever systems, a given barbell may feel lighter in one position and heavier in another position. Every

Figure 5–6 Barbells and dumbbells provide both positive resistance and negative resistance.

free-weight exercise has a sticking point, the place in the range of movement at which the mechanical factors are least favorable and the greatest amount of muscle force is required. It is the point where the exerciser succeeds or fails in making the lift.

For example, in the bench press exercise the sticking point is near the chest, as illustrated in Figure 5–7. Greater muscular effort is required at this point in the bench press movement than at any other, due to the mechanical factors involved. In terms of training efficiency, the heaviest barbell one can bench press (1RM weightload) actually produces maximum muscular stress at only one point in the entire range of move-

Figure 5–7 Approximate position in which the greatest muscular force is required when performing the bench press exercise.

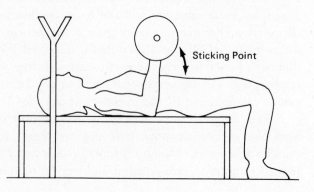

Sticking Point

ment. Once the barbell is pressed beyond the sticking point, less muscular effort is required to complete the lift, because the body's lever arrangements become more favorable. Consequently, movements that
incorporate a fixed resistance necessarily produce different levels of muscle stress at different points in the range of movement. For further
information on barbells and dumbbells see Appendix A.

Universal Gym Equipment

Universal Gym equipment has popularized traditional weight training by making it safe, convenient, space efficient, and time efficient.
(See Figure 5–8.) The Universal Gym includes a number of exercise
stations at which smooth running weight stacks are lifted by lever and
pully attachments. Because the weights travel on fixed tracks away from
the exerciser, spotters are not necessary, and the possibility of being
injured by a falling weight is greatly reduced.

The Universal Gym, although a relatively heavy piece of equipment,

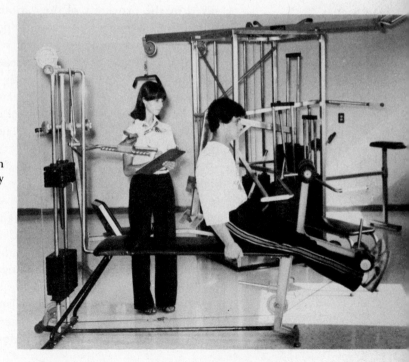

Figure 5–8 Universal Gym strength
training equipment with automatically
variable resistance feature.

can be easily moved from place to place by a single person. Once located, the Universal Gym becomes a one-stop training center, with stations for bench presses, lat bar pull-downs, overhead presses, curls, triceps press-downs, upright rows, seated rows, shoulder shrugs, leg presses, toe raises, situps, back hyperextensions, pull-ups, hanging knee-ups, dips, and a variety of improvised exercises. An additional piece of Universal Gym equipment enables the exerciser to perform leg extensions, leg curls, forearm exercises, and neck exercises.

Both pieces of Universal Gym equipment can be safely and comfortably placed in a small room or in a corner of the regular weight training facility. The stations are designed to minimize space requirements, and yet permit several persons to exercise concurrently. Because the Universal Gym is a self-contained unit, additional space for storing weight plates, bars, and exercise attachments is unnecessary.

Another aspect of the Universal Gym that has made it a popular training apparatus is the quick and effortless method of changing weight-loads. By simply removing and reinserting a steel pin, one can change the exercise weightload by several hundred pounds, a process that would require considerable time and effort with free weights. Time is also saved by the proximity of the various exercise stations to each other. The Universal Gym is well-suited for persons who prefer to do a sequence of different exercises with as little rest between exercises as possible.

Until recently, the numerous exercise stations, the small space requirements, and the safe and easily adjusted weight stacks were the key features of Universal Gym equipment. However, the newer Universal Gym models now provide automatically variable resistance at some of the exercise stations, which has certain advantages over fixed resistance training.

As previously indicated, muscles are capable of handling more weight at some points in the range of movement than others due to leverage factors. In the bench press exercise, for example, the muscles can handle progressively more weight as the arms become more fully extended. In other words, the muscles are capable of overcoming more resistance in Position B of Figure 5–9 than in Position A. Similarly, the muscles are capable of handling greater resistance in Position C of Figure 5–9 than in Position B.

With this in mind, the new Universal Gym bench press station automatically increases the resistance as the arms are extended. This is accomplished by moving the position of the resistance along the lifting

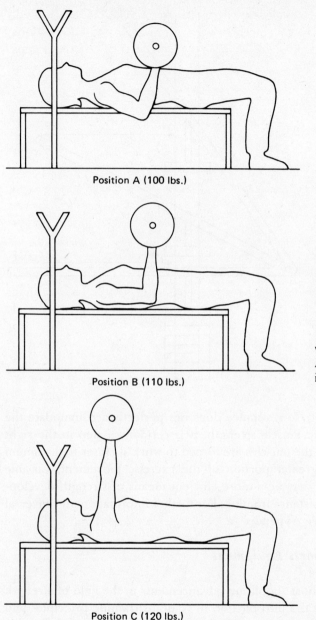

Position A (100 lbs.)

Position B (110 lbs.)

Position C (120 lbs.)

Figure 5–9 Due to leverage factors, the muscles are capable of handling greater resistance in the bench press exercise as the arms become more fully extended. Note that the hypothetical lifter is capable of handling more weight in Position B than in Position A, and more weight in Position C than in Position B.

lever. (See Figure 5–10.) Thus, leverage changes in the machine provide greater effective resistance at the same time that leverage changes in the body provide greater effective muscle force. Although this method

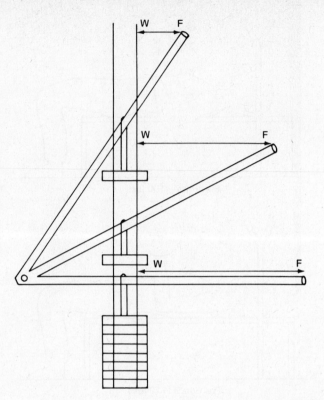

Figure 5–10 Schematic diagram illustrating how automatically variable resistance can be provided by a moving resistance on the lifting lever. As the lever is moved upward, the distance between the applied force (F) and the weightload (W) decreases, increasing the effective resistance.

of varying the exercise resistance does not perfectly accommodate the changes in effective muscle strength, it is certainly a step in the right direction. Because the muscles are forced to work at closer to maximum levels through a greater portion of the exercise movement, variable resistance training may be a more efficient means of strength development than fixed resistance training. For further information on Universal Gym equipment see Appendix A.

Nautilus Sports Equipment

Perhaps the most significant advancements in the field of strength training have been the introduction of Nautilus training principles and Nautilus training equipment. (See Figure 5–11.) Of the ten Nautilus training principles, three are unique to the design of Nautilus equipment. These are: 1) rotary movement, 2) direct resistance, and 3) automatically variable resistance.

Figure 5–11 Nautilus strength training machines feature rotary movement, direct resistance, and automatically variable resistance.

Rotary Movement. Almost all movements in the human body involve the rotation of a bone about a joint. Movements about the ankle joint, knee joint, hip joint, shoulder joint, elbow joint, and wrist joint all involve rotary movements. Yet, with few exceptions (e.g., bench curls, leg extensions, leg curls), most barbell and Universal Gym exercises require one to push or pull a resistance in a straight line. Squats, bench presses, lat bar pull-downs, and standing presses all involve linear movement of the resistance. Many Nautilus machines are designed to apply resistance in a rotary manner, with the machine's axis of rotation directly in line with the joint being used.

For example, the latissimus muscles move the upper arms from a position overhead to a position against the sides. With conventional barbells, the most common exercise for the latissimus muscles is bent rowing. Bent rowing involves a restricted range of joint motion (about 90 degrees), and linear movement of the barbell. (See Figure 5–12.)

With Universal Gym equipment the usual exercise for the latissimus muscles is the lat bar pull-down. Although lat bar pull-downs provide a greater range of motion than bent rowing (approximately 180 degrees), they too involve only linear movement of the lat bar and cable. (See Figure 5–13.)

The Nautilus Pull-over Machine provides both an extended range of motion (over 240 degrees) and rotary movement about the shoulder

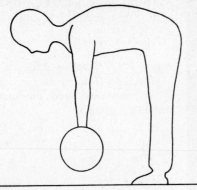

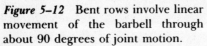

Figure 5–12 Bent rows involve linear movement of the barbell through about 90 degrees of joint motion.

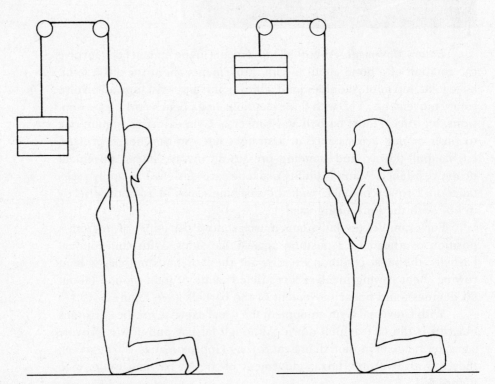

Figure 5–13 Lat bar pull-downs involve linear movement of the lat bar through approximately 180 degrees of joint motion.

joint. (See Figure 5–14.) In this exercise, both the upper arms and the resistance lever move through the same circular path as they rotate around the shoulder axis. This rotary action puts the resistive force in direct opposition to the movement force through the entire range of motion. The bent row and lat bar pull-down, on the other hand, provide resistance only in the vertical plane. In these exercises, the resistive force is in direct opposition to the movement force for a relatively small segment of the exercise movement (i.e., when the upper arms are approximately parallel to the floor). Although research evidence is lacking, it may be that rotary movement exercises provide a safer and more efficient means of strength development than exercises that provide resistance in only one plane.

   Direct Resistance. Direct resistance implies that the resistive force is applied to the same body segment to which the movement force is applied. For example, the latissimus muscles are attached to the upper arm, and their function is to pull the upper arms toward the sides of

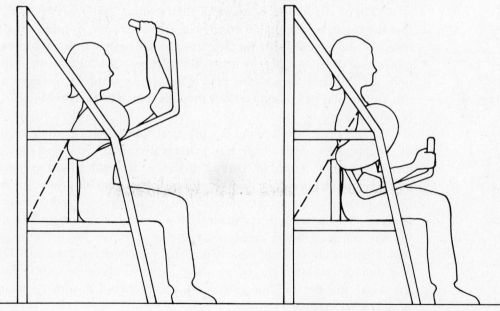

Figure 5–14 Nautilus pull-overs involve rotary movement of the pull-over bar (around the same axis as the shoulder joint) through more than 240 degrees of joint motion.

the body. If one were to provide direct resistance to the latissimus muscles, the resistive force would have to be applied to the upper arms.

As illustrated in Figure 5–12 this is not the case with conventional barbell training. The resistance in the bent row exercise is applied to the lower arms (hands) rather than to the upper arms. Execution of the exercise involves flexion of the elbow joint, which is a function of the biceps muscles. Stated differently, the bent row exercise cannot be completed without the elbow flexion made possible by the biceps. Consequently, if the smaller biceps muscles become fatigued, the bent rows must be discontinued even though the larger latissimus muscles may not have been fully stressed.

A similar situation exists with lat bar pull-downs on the Universal Gym. (See Figure 5–13.) The resistance is applied to the lower arms (hands) rather than to the upper arms. As with bent rows, execution of lat bar pull-downs involves flexion of the elbow joint, which is a function of the biceps muscles. If the weaker biceps muscles become fatigued, the lat bar pull-downs must be discontinued even though the stronger latissimus muscles may not have been fully stressed.

One of the unique features of the Nautilus Pull-over Machine is that the resistance is applied directly to the upper arm. In other words, both the movement force provided by the latissimus muscles and the movement resistance provided by the weight stack act upon the same body part. Because no assisting muscle groups are involved, the exercise can and should be continued until the latissimus muscles become completely fatigued.

Direct resistance training is a practical application of the Principle of Training Specificity. Exercises that involve more than one muscle group (two joint movements) tend to stress the smaller muscle group to a greater degree than they stress the larger muscle group. If the larger muscle group is prevented from being fully stressed, it is not likely to develop strength as efficiently as it could. For this reason, Nautilus has designed direct resistance exercise machines for the muscles that move the upper arms, namely the latissimus muscles, chest muscles, and shoulder muscles. Direct resistance exercises should continue until the target muscles become exhausted, which should in turn stimulate desirable strength adaptations.

Variable Resistance. Because changes in lever arrangements are basic to human movement, there are stronger positions and weaker positions in every range of joint movement. Consequently, a barbell that provides maximum resistance at the weakest point in an exercise movement offers less than maximum resistance at all other points in the movement. As previously discussed, Universal Gym equipment incorporates a lever arm with a movable resistance to compensate for leverage changes in the body. While this means of producing variable resistance works reasonably well with the bench press exercise, it is not applicable to exercises such as lat bar pull-downs, curls, triceps press-downs, rows, leg curls, leg extensions, and other exercises that do not involve a horizontal lever arm.

The variable resistance approach developed by Nautilus utilizes an oval shaped cam to automatically change the resistance throughout the range of movement. The cam is designed to accommodate the strength curve of the average person for a particular exercise. The strength curve represents the changes in effective muscle strength that one experiences during a given full-range movement. For example, the cam provides greater resistance during the latter part of the biceps curl than during the first part of the biceps curl, which is consistent with the strength curve for this particular arm movement. If a circular wheel were used, the distance from the axis of rotation to the point where the chain leaves the wheel would not change, the mechanics of the system would not be altered, and the resistance would stay the same throughout the entire range of movement. (See Figure 5–15.) However, the oval shape of the Nautilus cam changes the distance from the axis of rotation to the point where the chain leaves the cam. This changes the mechanics of the system and produces a corresponding variation in resistance throughout the movement range. (See Figure 5–16.) More specifically, as the distance from the axis of rotation to the chain increases, the resistance increases. Conversely, as the distance from the axis of rotation to the chain decreases, the resistance decreases.

Although the shape of the Nautilus cam is based on an average strength curve for each of the exercise movements, it produces a relatively constant stress on the muscles throughout the range of motion. The resistance does not feel lighter in some positions than in others. The use of cams designed for specific movement patterns appears to be both an effective and practical means of providing automatically variable resistance. Variable resistance training may be a more efficient method of strength development than fixed resistance training, because it theoretically requires maximum muscular effort through the entire range of movement, rather than only at the sticking point. For further information on Nautilus Sports machines see Appendix A.

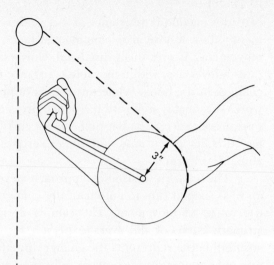

Figure 5–15   A circular wheel does not change the distance from the axis of rotation to the chain at the point where it leaves the wheel. The resistance therefore remains the same through the entire range of movement.

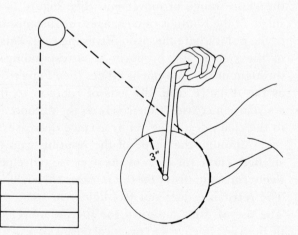

Comparison of Training Equipment

If one were interested in strengthening the latissimus muscles, and had only a barbell and weights, the best exercise would probably be

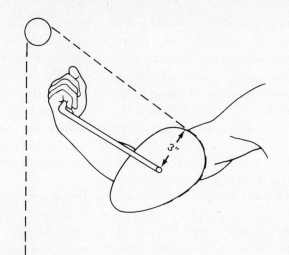

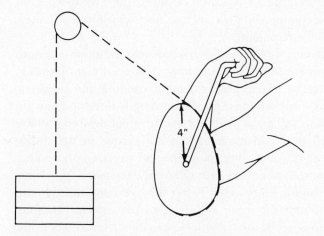

Figure 5–16 An oval-shaped cam changes the distance from the axis of rotation to the chain at the point where it leaves the cam. This changes the mechanical advantage and varies the resistance accordingly throughout the range of movement.

bent rows. Bent rows apply the Stress Adaptation Principle through a limited (90 degrees) range of movement. If that same person had access to Universal Gym equipment, the best exercise would most likely be lat bar pull-downs. Lat bar pull-downs apply the Stress Adaptation Principle through a greater (180 degrees) range of movement. Neither of these exercises, however, makes provision for rotary movement, direct resistance, or automatically variable resistance. Consequently, if one had access to Nautilus equipment, the best exercise would probably be Nautilus Machine pull-overs. Nautilus Machine pull-overs apply the stress adaptation principle through a full 240 degrees of shoulder rotation. In addition, they provide rotary movement, direct resistance, and automatically variable resistance. Although research evidence is lacking, it seems that each of these training features would facilitate strength development in the latissimus muscles.

Of course there are advantages and disadvantages to every type of strength training program. Two very important considerations in the selection of training equipment are cost and convenience. Barbells are relatively inexpensive and allow persons to train at home, at a time of their own choosing. Universal Gym equipment is ideal for schools, colleges, and clubs, but may pose both financial and spatial problems to the typical at home strength training enthusiast. The numerous pieces of Nautilus equipment with their special training features make an impressive strength training center. However, the relatively high cost and large space requirements of Nautilus machines are prohibitive for most schools and colleges. Although many universities and professional athletic teams have well-equipped Nautilus facilities, the average person would need to visit a commercial gym, such as a Nautilus Fitness Center, to train with Nautilus equipment.

There is no question that people have developed great strength and excellent physiques with barbell training, Universal Gym training, and Nautilus training, as well as with isokinetic training and isometric training. As long as the basic principles of strength development are followed, most persons will make progress towards their desired training objectives. Although time and money are major factors in the choice of training equipment, the most important aspect of any strength training program is enjoyment. Experiment with different exercises and various pieces of strength training equipment. Select the exercises and training equipment that you enjoy the most, and design a personalized training program. The key to success in strength development, as in any other endeavor, is hard work, but that hard work should be enjoyable.

Chapter Six

Strength Training Exercises

EXERCISES FOR BARBELLS AND DUMBBELLS

Exercises performed with barbells and dumbbells are often referred to as free-weight exercises because the movement pathways are determined by the exerciser rather than by a machine. That is, the exerciser is free to manipulate the weights in the desired manner, without following a fixed movement pattern.

Although there are newer, and probably more efficient, ways to develop muscular strength, barbells and dumbbells remain the preferred mode of training for most strength enthusiasts, as well as for competitive weightlifters and bodybuilders. Perhaps one reason for the popularity of free-weight training is the feeling of accomplishment one experiences from controlling the movement of a mass of iron. There are few things as satisfying to a weight trainer as taking a heavy barbell from the bench press standards, lowering it to the chest, and pressing it back up to full arm's extension.

Another reason for the widespread use of barbells and dumbbells is undoubtedly financial. Although many schools and colleges are equipped with various types of strength training machines, the average individual cannot afford expensive apparatus or club memberships. Consequently, dumbbells and barbells are found in most home gyms.

A third reason for the success of barbell/dumbbell training is versatility. There are several different free-weight exercises that can be performed for every major muscle group. In the following section, over 60 free-weight exercises for the ten major muscle groups are presented and described. When performed in a slow and controlled manner, each of these exercises is an effective means for developing strength in the prime mover muscle groups.

BREATHING DURING EXERCISE

Before experimenting with various strength training exercises, one should understand something about breathing during forceful muscular contraction. By taking a deep breath and holding it while straining to complete a repetition, an exerciser can actually shut down the blood flow to an area of the body.

For example, the carotid arteries in the front of the neck are primarily responsible for supplying blood and oxygen to the brain. The inside pressure created by breath holding coupled with the outside pressure of tightly contracted neck muscles during a maximum effort standing press may be sufficient to limit the flow of blood through these arteries. This could lead to a feeling of lightheadedness or an actual loss of consciousness due to lack of oxygen to the brain cells.

Perhaps more important, the increased pressure in the chest area that results from holding the breath during a strenuous lifting movement can interfere with venous blood return to the heart and significantly elevate blood pressure. This undesirable reaction is known as the Valsalva Response. Consequently, the breath should never be held for a prolonged period of time when exercising with weights.

On the other hand, many exercises require the chest area to be stabilized for successful execution. Consequently, for maximum performance in exercises such as the bench press, breathing must cease momentarily. The key is to never hold the breath for more than a moment, and to breathe on *every* repetition.

From a physiological standpoint, the best system of breathing requires the exerciser to inhale during the lowering movement (eccentric contraction) and to exhale during the lifting movement (concentric contraction). In this manner, the internal pressure is decreased as the external pressure is increased. The opposite pattern of breathing causes the internal pressure and external pressure to increase simultaneously and should be avoided.

Most exercisers develop a breathing pattern that suits their particular training style without jeopardizing blood flow or restricting their oxygen supply. As long as one does not take deep breaths or attempt to hold the breath for more than a moment, problems should not be encountered.

EXERCISES FOR THE CHEST

The pectoralis major muscles of the chest are the prime mover muscle group for shoulder horizontal flexion. Consequently, most chest exercises involve forward movement of the arms, with the arms at right angles to the chest.

Barbell Bench Press

Probably the most widely used exercise for the chest muscles is the barbell bench press. (See Figure 6–1.) The bench press actually utilizes three major muscle groups, the pectoralis major, the anterior deltoids, and the triceps. The bench press is performed on a flat bench, usually equipped with standards on which to place the barbell.

The exerciser begins by lifting the barbell from the standards and holding it at full arm's extension. The barbell is lowered slowly to the chest, and pressed back up to full arm's extension. The head, shoulders,

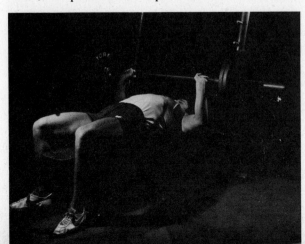

Figure 6–1 Barbell Bench Press

and buttocks should remain in contact with the bench throughout the exercise. A wide grip places more emphasis on the chest muscles, whereas a narrow grip makes greater use of the triceps muscles.

Dumbbell Bench Press

There are several variations to the bench press exercise. Many people prefer to use dumbbells rather than a barbell because the arms can be lowered farther, enabling a greater range of movement. (See Figure 6–2.) A partner is usually necessary to hand the dumbbells to the exerciser. For optimal results in this exercise, the elbows should be away from the body and pointed outward. As with barbell bench presses, the dumbbells should be raised and lowered perpendicular to the body.

Figure 6–2 Dumbbell Bench Press

Barbell Incline Press

Bench presses can also be performed on an incline bench and are then generally referred to as incline presses. (See Figure 6–3.) Incline presses involve the same major muscle groups, but the emphasis is somewhat different. Whereas bench presses primarily affect the lower and mid-chest area, incline presses place greater stress on the upper chest and shoulders.

The lifting procedures for the incline press are similar to those for the bench press. The barbell is first lifted from the standards and

Figure 6–3 Barbell Incline Press

held at full arm's extension. It is then lowered slowly to the upper chest, and pressed back up to full arm's extension. It is important to keep the barbell in the vertical plane throughout the exercise.

Dumbbell Incline Press

Dumbbells can also be used for incline presses. (See Figure 6–4.) The movement pattern is exactly the same. The dumbbells should be raised and lowered in the vertical plane, and held perpendicular to the body. An advantage of using dumbbells is the greater range of movement that is possible. The need for a training partner to place the dumbbells in the exerciser's hands may be considered a disadvantage, but partners (spotters) are just as necessary for the barbell versions of bench and incline presses in case the exerciser cannot complete the lift.

Figure 6–4 Dumbbell Incline Press

Figure 6–5 Dumbbell Flies

Dumbbell Fly

Another chest exercise that utilizes a bench is known as a dumbbell fly. (See Figure 6–5.) A flat bench is normally used, but the exercise can also be performed on an incline bench. The exerciser lies on the bench and holds the dumbbells at full arm's extension, directly above the chest. The arms are slowly lowered away from the sides, and the elbows are allowed to bend slightly as they approach the bottom of the movement range. The arms are then raised back up to the starting position. The upper arms should remain at right angles to the body throughout the lifting and lowering movements. Because leverage factors play a significant role in dumbbell flies, relatively light dumbbells must be used if this exercise is to be performed slowly and safely. The arms should be lowered far enough to place a stretch on the chest muscles, but certainly not to the point of discomfort.

Cross-Chest Pull

A chest exercise quite similar to dumbbell flies can be performed with pulley weights. This exercise, simply called cross-chest pulls, begins with the arms outstretched in a T-position. (See Figure 6–6.) The arms are brought to the front of the body in a downward-forward movement, held momentarily, and returned slowly to the starting position. A slight

Figure 6–6 Cross-Chest Pull

bend at the elbows is recommended to prevent excessive stress on the joints due to leverage factors.

Unlike dumbbell flies, cross-chest pulls involve the back muscles (latissimus dorsi) as well as the chest muscles. This is due to the shoulder adduction movement that characterizes this exercise. One advantage of cross-chest pulls over other chest exercises is the greater range of movement that is possible at the completion of the pull. The arms can be pulled past the midline of the body to permit full contraction of the chest muscles. If the exerciser so desires, cross-chest pulls can be performed one arm at a time.

Bar Dip

Bar dips provide an excellent training stimulus for the chest, as well as for several other major muscle groups. (See Figure 6–7.) When performed correctly, bar dips involve the pectoralis major, latissimus dorsi, anterior deltoids, and triceps muscles. Care must be taken to maintain the body in a vertical position, and to avoid swinging during the exercise. The exerciser begins by jumping to a support position on the bars with the arms fully extended. The body is slowly lowered as far as possible, then pressed back up to full arm's extension. To obtain a reasonable range of movement, the upper arms should be at least parallel to the floor in the down position. Resistance can be progressively increased by attaching barbell plates to a rope tied around the waist.

Figure 6–7 Bar Dip

EXERCISES FOR THE BACK

The latissimus dorsi muscles of the back are the prime mover muscle group for shoulder adduction, shoulder extension, and shoulder horizontal extension. Most back exercises, therefore, involve downward or backward movement of the arms. Although there are a variety of exercises that place stress on the latissimus muscles, those that begin with the arms fully extended overhead seem to be the most effective.

Lat Bar Pull-down

Lat bar pull-downs provide an excellent training stimulus for the back muscles. (See Figures 6–8 and 6–9.) This exercise is generally performed from a kneeling or sitting position directly under the pull-down bar. Beginning with the arms fully extended overhead, the bar is pulled to the upper chest, held momentarily, and returned slowly to the starting position. Lat bar pull-downs involve the latissimus muscles and the biceps muscles. However, the role of the biceps muscles is partly dependent upon the grip one utilizes. A wide-spaced, palms away grip places less emphasis on the biceps, whereas a narrow-spaced, palms facing grip places greater emphasis on the biceps.

As the weightload increases, it becomes necessary to secure the body to the floor. This can be done by hooking the heels under a barbell or by having a partner press down on the shoulders during the exercise.

Figure 6–8 Lat Bar Pull-down—Wide

Figure 6–9 Lat Bar Pull-down—Narrow

Pull-up

Pull-ups provide essentially the same training stimulus for the back muscles as lat bar pull-downs. (See Figures 6–10 and 6–11.) In fact, the only difference is that pull-downs bring the bar to the body, whereas pull-ups bring the body to the bar. Pull-ups involve the latissimus dorsi muscles and the biceps muscles. As with lat bar pull-downs, a narrow-spaced, palms facing grip utilizes the biceps muscles to a greater degree than a wide-spaced, palms away grip.

It is recommended that front pull-ups be performed to provide maximum range of movement. Each repetition should begin from a full hang, and proceed until the chest makes contact with the bar. After a momentary pause, the body should be lowered slowly until the arms are completely extended. It is important to keep the body from swinging, because swinging reduces the effectiveness of the exercise.

Figure 6–10 Pull-up—Narrow

Figure 6–11 Pull-up—Wide

If one's bodyweight is too heavy to permit a single repetition, a chair can be used to reach the top (arms flexed) position. The muscles can then be trained eccentrically by resisting the downward movement of the body. If one's bodyweight is too light, resistance can easily be added by attaching weights to a rope slung over the hips.

Barbell Bent Row

Bent rows provide a reasonably good training stimulus for the back muscles. (See Figures 6–12 and 6–13.) The principal muscle groups affected by this exercise are the latissimus dorsi, biceps, and posterior deltoids. As the name implies, this exercise is performed from a bent over position, with the back parallel to the floor. Beginning at full arm's extension, the exerciser brings the barbell to the chest, pauses momentarily, and slowly lowers the barbell to the starting position. The bar may be held with a wide grip and pulled to the chest, or held with a narrow grip and pulled to the stomach. Both methods are effective, although the latter technique places slightly greater emphasis on the latissimus muscles.

Due to the mechanics of this exercise, considerable stress is placed on the lower back musculature. This potentially harmful stress to the lower back area can be significantly reduced simply by resting the forehead on an appropriately sized bench during the exercise. Because form is an important factor in performing bent rows, it is recommended that each set be terminated when the barbell can no longer be lifted all the way to the chest.

Figure 6–13 Bent Row—Supported

Figure 6–12 Bent Row—Unsupported

Figure 6–14   Dumbbell Bent Row

Dumbbell Bent Row

Bent rows can also be performed with dumbbells. (See Figure 6–14.) The basic movement is identical to that done with a barbell and, of course, involves the same muscle groups. Beginning from a hanging position, the dumbbell is lifted to the torso, held momentarily, and slowly returned to full arm's extension. Dumbbell bent rows offer the following advantages over their barbell counterparts. First, the use of dumbbells enables a greater range of movement. Second, the exercise can be performed with one arm at a time. Third, the non-exercising arm can be placed on a bench to provide stability and reduce the stress on the lower back. As with the barbell version of this exercise, the latissimus muscles receive a slightly greater training effect when the elbows are kept close to the body during the lifting and lowering movements.

Seated Row

The seated row is basically a bent row performed from a sitting position. (See Figure 6–15.) The use of a double pulley apparatus allows the resistance to act in the horizontal plane. The exerciser sits in front of the pulley, braces the feet against the apparatus, and grasps the bar with the preferred grip. Beginning with the arms fully extended to the

Figure 6–15   Seated Row

front, the exerciser pulls the bar to the chest, pauses momentarily, and slowly returns to the starting position.

Like the other rowing-type exercises, seated rows involve the latissimus dorsi, biceps, and posterior deltoids. Because a wide grip places slightly greater emphasis on the posterior deltoid muscles, a narrow grip may be preferred. If individual hand grips are attached to the cable, the movement range can be increased. Seated rows are somewhat easier on the lower back than bent rows are, because the torso remains in a vertical position throughout the exercise.

Barbell Pull-over

Barbell pull-overs provide a training stimulus for the latissimus muscles, as well as the posterior deltoids and the triceps. (See Figure 6–16.) This exercise is performed from a back-lying position on a flat bench. The barbell is first placed on the chest with the hands about shoulder width apart. It is then lifted over the face and allowed to pull the arms towards the floor. When the arms are stretched as far as possible without discomfort, the exerciser lifts the barbell over the face to the chest. This is the concentric phase of the exercise.

Although barbell pull-overs may initially feel awkward, they usually improve shoulder girdle flexibility and become easier to perform after a few training sessions.

The major disadvantage of barbell pull-overs is the relatively short distance that the resistance is moved in the vertical plane (i.e., against gravity). Although it is obviously important to clear the face with the barbell, this phase of the movement does not place maximum stress on the latissimus muscles.

Figure 6–16   Barbell Pull-over

Figure 6–17 Dumbbell Pull-over

Dumbbell Pull-over

Pull-overs can be performed as easily with a dumbbell as with a barbell. (See Figure 6–17.) Dumbbell pull-overs are often done with the arms straight rather than bent. Straight arm pull-overs must be done with a relatively light dumbbell due to the leverage factors involved. This exercise begins with the dumbbell at full arm's extension directly above the chest. The dumbbell is slowly lowered behind the head as far as possible without discomfort. It is then lifted with straight arms back up to the starting position.

Many people use dumbbell pull-overs as a stretching exercise for the chest and abdominal muscles, as well as a strengthening exercise for the latissimus dorsi, posterior deltoids, and triceps muscles.

EXERCISES FOR THE SHOULDERS

The deltoid muscles that cover the shoulder joints are involved in practically all movements of the upper arms. The anterior deltoid, middle deltoid, and posterior deltoid all contribute to shoulder abduction. The anterior head is further responsible for shoulder flexion, and the posterior head is also involved in shoulder extension.

Many shoulder exercises include all three parts of the deltoid muscles, as well as the upper section of the trapezius muscle. These exercises in which shoulder abduction is the dominant movement are generally recommended for overall shoulder development.

Barbell Press

The standing barbell press is a basic shoulder exercise that, when performed correctly, stresses all three heads of the deltoids, the upper trapezius muscles, and the triceps. (See Figure 6–18.) The barbell press may be executed from a standing or sitting position. In either case, the back should remain straight throughout the exercise. Leaning backward or arching the back changes the emphasis of the exercise, and may place excessive stress on the lower back area.

The barbell press is initiated from the shoulder rest position. Unless lifting standards are available, the bar must first be cleaned to the shoulders. (See Power Clean.) Once the bar is at shoulder level, the exerciser presses the bar directly overhead to full arm's extension. The bar is held briefly in the lockout position, then lowered slowly back to the shoulders. Although bringing the bar behind the neck generally produces stricter lifting form, many people experience shoulder discomfort when this is done. It is recommended that a relatively wide grip be used to emphasize the shoulder abduction movement.

Figure 6–18   Barbell Press

Figure 6–19 Dumbbell Press

Figure 6–20 Alternate Dumbbell Press

Dumbbell Press

There are at least two reasons dumbbells may be preferred to barbells for performing shoulder presses. (See Figures 6–19 and 6–20.) First, dumbbells permit greater freedom of movement, and facilitate the desired shoulder abduction movement. Second, dumbbell presses can be performed in an alternate (one arm at a time) manner. This results in a side-bend reaction rather than the potentially dangerous back-bend reaction typically produced by two-arm presses.

Whichever method is used, the pressing movement is essentially the same. Once the dumbbells have been cleaned to the shoulders, they are pressed to full arm's extension, held momentarily, and slowly lowered back to the shoulder rest position. When performed alternately, the left arm should begin its upward movement as the right arm completes its downward movement, and vice versa.

Barbell Incline Press

The barbell incline press is often substituted for the barbell press. (See Figure 6–21.) Although this exercise primarily stresses the front head of the deltoids, along with the upper chest and triceps, it permits the exerciser to handle heavier weightloads and provides support for the back. If an adjustable bench is available, the higher inclines place greater emphasis on the shoulder muscles, whereas the lower inclines place greater emphasis on the chest muscles.

133

Figure 6–21 Barbell Incline Press

The exerciser begins by lifting the barbell from the standards and holding it at full arm's extension. The barbell is then lowered slowly to the chest, and pressed back up to full arm's extension. All of the lifting and lowering movements should occur in the vertical plane. A wide grip is recommended to emphasize the shoulder abduction movement.

Dumbbell Incline Press

Dumbbell incline presses are similar to barbell incline presses, but permit a greater range of movement and facilitate shoulder abduction. (See Figure 6–22.) This exercise involves the deltoids (primarily the anterior head), upper chest, and triceps.

Beginning at the shoulder rest position with the elbows pointed

Figure 6–22 Dumbbell Incline Press

away from the sides, the dumbbells are pressed to full arm's extension, held momentarily, and returned slowly back to the shoulders. As with the barbell version of this exercise, the dumbbells should only be moved in the vertical plane.

Upright Row

Although many shoulder exercises involve pressing movements, it is not necessary to raise weights overhead to stress the deltoid muscles. Upright rows provide an excellent training stimulus for all three heads of the deltoids, as well as for the upper trapezius muscles. (See Figure 6–23.)

This exercise begins with the barbell at waist level and the hands very close together. The barbell is then lifted straight up to chin level by bringing the elbows upward and outward as far as possible. After a momentary pause, the barbell is slowly lowered to the starting position.

Because the weights are not lifted above the head, this exercise does not produce a back lean or create pressure in the neck area. Because upright rows are as effective as presses but do not endanger the lower back area, they may be the preferred exercise for shoulder development.

Figure 6–23 Upright Row

Figure 6–24 Dumbbell Lateral Raise

Dumbbell Lateral Raise

The dumbbell lateral raise is perhaps the most direct way to stress the shoulder muscles. (See Figure 6–24.) This shoulder abduction exercise affects all three heads of the deltoids, and the upper trapezius.

The exerciser begins with the dumbbells at the sides. The arms are then lifted straight up until they are parallel with the floor and form a T-position with the body. After a momentary pause the dumbbells are slowly lowered back down to the sides.

Due to the significant leverage disadvantage inherent in this exercise, very light dumbbells are usually sufficient to produce the desired training effect. If discomfort is experienced in the elbow joint, it is recommended that the arms be held in a slightly flexed position during the exercise.

Shoulder Shrug

The shoulder shrug provides a direct training stimulus for the upper trapezius muscle. (See Figure 6–25.) Although it has limited effect on the deltoids, the shoulder shrug is an important exercise for shoulder girdle strength and stability. Due to the strength of the upper trapezius muscle, a relatively heavy barbell is generally used for this exercise.

The shoulder shrug is a simple movement involving elevation of the shoulder girdle. As the name implies, one merely brings the shoul-

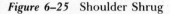

Figure 6–25 Shoulder Shrug

ders towards the ears in a shrugging manner while holding a barbell at waist level. Because the range of movement is somewhat restricted, a momentary pause at the completion of each repetition is advisable. It is recommended that the lifting and lowering movements be performed slowly, and with the arms straight to provide maximum stress on the upper trapezius muscles.

EXERCISES FOR THE TRICEPS

The triceps muscles of the upper arm are responsible for elbow extension. Although the triceps play a major role in all pressing movements (e.g., bench press, incline press, standing press), most triceps exercises attempt to isolate this muscle group by stabilizing the upper arms. Consequently, triceps exercises typically involve a fixed elbow position and rotary movement of the lower arms.

Triceps Press-down

The press-down exercise utilizes a pulley system to enable the triceps to work against gravity from a standing position. (See Figure 6–26.) Although the chest and back muscles stabilize the position of

Figure 6–26 Triceps Press-down

the upper arms, the press-down movement is actually accomplished by the triceps.

The exerciser begins by taking an overhand grip on the press-down bar and bringing it to about neck level. In this position, the elbows should be pressed against the sides and the arms should be fully flexed. The concentric phase of the movement requires the exerciser to extend the arms downward without changing the position of the elbows. After a momentary pause, the arms are slowly returned to the starting position (eccentric phase). It is important to keep the body straight and the upper arms stationary throughout the exercise.

Barbell Lying Triceps Extension

The barbell lying triceps extension provides an excellent training stimulus for the triceps muscles when performed correctly. (See Figure 6–27.) The keys to this exercise are a relatively narrow hand spacing and a minimum amount of upper arm movement.

The exerciser assumes a lying position on the bench or floor, and holds the barbell at full arm's extension above the chest. Without changing the position of the elbows, the exerciser lowers the barbell until it almost touches the forehead. The lowering movement (eccentric phase) must be performed in a slow and controlled manner for obvious reasons.

138

Figure 6–27 Barbell Lying Triceps Extension

The barbell is then returned to the starting position by extending the lower arms.

It is important to keep the elbows high throughout the exercise. This is accomplished by isometric contraction of the chest and shoulder muscles. If the elbows are allowed to drop, the chest and shoulders assume a major role in the exercise (similar to the bench press), and the contribution of the triceps muscles is correspondingly reduced. It is recommended that an angled bar be used for this exercise to reduce stress on the wrists.

Dumbbell Lying Triceps Extension

The lying triceps extension can also be performed with a dumbbell. (See Figure 6–28.) The only difference between this exercise and the barbell version is that the dumbbell is held at full arm's extension above the face and lowered to a position beside the head. The elbows should remain high throughout the exercise, and upper arm movement should be minimized as much as possible. Although the dumbbell lying triceps extension is sometimes combined with the dumbbell pull-over (pull-over-extension), this tends to be a less effective exercise for triceps development due to the momentum generated during the first part of the movement.

Figure 6–28 Dumbbell Lying Triceps Extension

Figure 6–29   French Press

French Press

The French press is actually a triceps extension performed from a standing or sitting position. (See Figure 6–29.) As in the lying triceps extension, the upper arms must remain in a fixed position to place maximum stress on the triceps muscles. Because of the leverage factors involved, it is recommended that this exercise be done with a dumbbell rather than a barbell.

The exerciser begins by holding the dumbbell above the head with the arms fully extended. The dumbbell is slowly lowered behind the neck without changing the position of the elbows. The lower arms are then extended back up to the starting position.

As long as the elbows are held high, the shoulder muscles act as stabilizers and the triceps muscles serve as prime movers. If the elbows are dropped, the role of the shoulder muscles increases while that of the triceps decreases.

Close-Grip Bench Press

One exercise that places great stress on the triceps muscles is the close-grip bench press. (See Figure 6–30.) Although this exercise also

Figure 6–30 Close-Grip Bench Press

involves the chest and shoulder muscles, the relatively heavy weightloads that can be utilized provide an excellent training stimulus for the triceps.

The exerciser grasps the barbell with a narrow grip and holds it at full arm's extension above the chest. The bar is slowly lowered to the chest, then pressed back up to the starting position. The elbows should remain about shoulder width apart throughout the lifting and lowering movements. This reduces the contribution of the chest muscles and places greater emphasis on the triceps.

The major difference between close-grip bench presses and standard bench presses is the movement pattern of the upper arms. In the close-grip version, the upper arms move parallel to the body (elbows in), whereas in the regular bench press, the upper arms move perpendicular to the body (elbows out). An angled bar may be preferred for this exercise to reduce stress on the wrists.

Chair Dip

Chair dips are a variation of bar dips that emphasize the triceps muscles. (See Figure 6–31.) This exercise requires no equipment other than a chair or bench, and can be made progressively more difficult by placing a barbell across the hips.

The exerciser sits on the edge of a chair with the legs extended and the hands placed next to the hips (fingers pointing downward). The starting position is assumed by extending the arms and moving the hips forward just far enough to clear the chair. The exerciser slowly lowers the hips to the floor, and presses back up to full arm's extension.

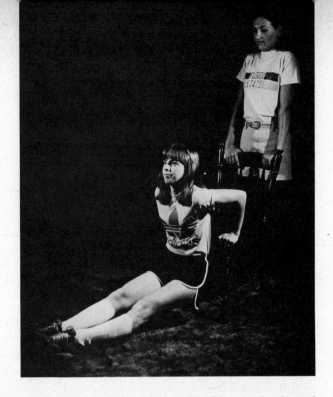

Figure 6–31   Chair Dip

The legs should remain straight, and the elbows should point backward throughout the exercise.

Although chair dips involve the chest, back, and shoulder muscles, major emphasis is placed on the triceps when the exercise is performed correctly. A variation of the chair dip is to place the feet on another chair rather than on the floor. This increases the stress on the triceps muscles, and makes it easier to keep a barbell across the hips.

EXERCISES FOR THE BICEPS

The biceps muscles of the upper arm are responsible for elbow flexion. The biceps work together with the back muscles on pulling exercises such as pull-downs, pull-ups, bent rows, and seated rows. However, a better training effect is obtained when the upper arms are stabilized, and the biceps are the prime mover muscle group. For this reason, most biceps exercises attempt to maintain the elbows in a fixed position.

Barbell Curl

One of the most popular biceps exercises is the barbell curl. (See Figure 6–32.) When performed correctly, this exercise emphasizes the

142

Figure 6-32 Barbell Curl

role of the biceps muscles, and enables the use of relatively heavy weight-loads. The key to obtaining desired results from barbell curls is to keep the upper arms stationary while the lower arms go through a full range of movement.

The exerciser begins by holding the barbell at full arm's extension with an underhand grip. Without changing the position of the elbows, the exerciser raises the barbell until the arms are completely flexed. The barbell is then lowered slowly back to the starting position.

It is important to keep the torso as straight as possible throughout the exercise to eliminate assisting body movements. It is also necessary to keep the upper arms against the sides to prevent the shoulder muscles from contributing to the movement. When barbell curls are executed in strict manner, the biceps are the prime mover muscles, and the chest and back muscles function as upper arm stabilizers. An angled bar is recommended for reducing stress on the wrists when performing this exercise.

Dumbbell Curl

Dumbbell curls are as effective as barbell curls for developing the biceps muscles. (See Figure 6–33.) Because dumbbells permit greater freedom of movement, the exerciser is unlikely to experience wrist pain when performing dumbbell curls.

Figure 6-33 Dumbbell Curl

Dumbbell curls involve essentially the same movement pattern as barbell curls. To be maximally effective, the upper arms must remain stationary while the lower arms move from full extension to full flexion. The lowering movement (eccentric contraction) must also be performed slowly for best results. As long as the torso does not bend and the elbows do not change position, the biceps muscles can obtain a substantial training effect from dumbbell curls.

Seated Dumbbell Curl

The major problem with standing curls is the tendency to lean backward and allow body movements to assist the biceps. One way to eliminate body sway is to do dumbbell curls from a sitting position. (See Figure 6–34.)

After assuming a sitting position on a narrow bench, the exerciser holds the dumbbells at full arm's extension. Without changing the posi-

Figure 6–34 Seated Dumbbell Curl

tion of the elbows, the exerciser raises the dumbbells until the arms are completely flexed. The dumbbells are then lowered slowly back to the starting position.

Because the seated dumbbell curl significantly reduces body movements, the biceps muscles are forced to do the majority of the work in this exercise. It is important, however, to hold the upper arms stationary throughout the exercise to place maximum stress on the biceps.

Barbell Bench Curl

Another way to isolate the biceps muscles is to perform curls on a specially designed bench. (See Figure 6–35.) Barbell bench curls eliminate both body sway and upper arm movement by means of a padded board beneath the elbows. It is interesting to note that much less weight can be curled in this exercise than in regular barbell curls, even when the latter are performed with strict technique.

Figure 6–35   Barbell Bench Curl

The exerciser sits on the bench and places the upper arms on the padded board. The barbell is taken from a partner, and held at full arm's extension with an underhand grip. It is then curled upward until the arms are completely flexed, and returned slowly back to the starting position.

Although barbell bench curls provide a large degree of control, the exerciser should sit erect and keep the chest in contact with the padded board during the lifting and lowering movements for best results. It is recommended that an angled bar be used for this exercise to reduce strain on the wrists.

Dumbbell Bench Curl

Bench curls can also be performed with dumbbells. (See Figure 6–36.) Dumbbell bench curls provide greater freedom of movement, and can be performed one arm at a time.

The exerciser sits on the bench, places the upper arm on the padded board, and holds the dumbbell at full arm's extension. Moving only the lower arm, the exerciser curls the dumbbell upward as far as possible, then returns it slowly to the starting position.

The dumbbell bench curl is a favorite exercise for persons who wish to isolate the biceps and intensify the training stimulus. Due to the strictness of this exercise, a relatively light dumbbell is sufficient to stress the biceps muscles.

Figure 6–37 Cable Bench Curl

Figure 6–36 Dumbbell Bench Curl

If desired, this exercise can also be performed with a cable, as indicated in Figure 6–37. Cable resistance is less affected by changes in arm position than is free-weight resistance.

Dumbbell Concentration Curl

The dumbbell concentration curl utilizes the inside of the thigh to stabilize the upper arm. (See Figure 6–38.) When executed correctly, this exercise provides almost as much control as the bench curl.

Dumbbell concentration curls are usually done from a sitting position. The exerciser simply places the elbow against the thigh and allows the arm to hang fully extended. Moving only the lower arm, the dumbbell is curled to the shoulder, then returned slowly back to the starting position.

For this exercise to be maximally effective, both the thigh and the torso must remain stationary throughout the lifting and lowering

Figure 6–38 Dumbbell Concentration
Curl

movements. Leaning backward during the final repetitions reduces the
stress on the biceps muscles, and should be avoided as much as possible.

Pull-up

The pull-up has previously been recommended as a useful exercise
for developing the latissimus muscles of the back. It is also an excellent
exercise for training the biceps. (See Figure 6–39.)

To place maximum stress on the biceps, the exerciser should grasp
the pull-up bar with an underhand grip, hands about shoulder width
apart. Beginning from a full hang, the body should be pulled upward
until the chest touches the bar. After a brief pause, the body should
be slowly lowered back to the starting position.

Although pull-ups involve the latissimus dorsi and the biceps, the
use of relatively heavy weightloads (i.e., bodyweight plus attached barbell
plates) make this an effective exercise for both muscle groups. It is

Figure 6–39 Pull-up—Narrow

important to avoid swinging when performing pull-ups. This is best accomplished by executing the lifting and lowering movements in a slow and controlled manner.

EXERCISES FOR THE LEGS

The leg muscles are the most powerful and frequently used muscles in the body. Of particular importance are the quadriceps muscles in the front of the thigh, and the hamstrings muscles in the back of the thigh. Although these muscle groups are antagonists, they work together in many exercises. The quadriceps are prime movers for knee extension and hip flexion, whereas the hamstrings are prime movers for knee flexion and hip extension. However, both muscle groups are involved in exercises that require simultaneous knee extension and hip extension, such as half squats, dumbbell jump squats, power cleans, vertical leg presses, seated leg presses, and dead lifts. While it is possible to stress both muscle groups with a single exercise, the quadriceps can be trained independently with leg extensions, and the hamstrings can be isolated with leg curls.

Exercises for the lower legs can be divided into two categories: those in which the ankles are extended stress the calf muscles, and those in which the ankles are flexed work the shin muscles.

Half Squat

The classic exercise for the legs is the half squat. (See Figure 6–40.) This exercise can be performed with relatively heavy weightloads, and requires only a lifting rack to support the barbell between lifts.

The exerciser begins by placing the barbell across the shoulders and lifting it off the supporting rack. The hands should be wide-spaced, and the feet should be about shoulder-width apart. The exerciser then lowers the body slowly to a half-squat position (thighs approximately parallel to the floor), and returns to a stand. It is important to keep the head up and the back straight at all times during the exercise for safety, balance, and control.

Due to the positioning of the barbell, it is imperative that a safety rack or spotter be utilized when performing this exercise. If discomfort is experienced in the shoulders or neck area, a towel may be wrapped around the bar to provide padding. A bench can be placed under the exerciser so that the movement range will remain consistent throughout the exercise. That is, the exerciser will not begin the lifting phase until the buttocks make contact with the bench.

Figure 6–40   Half Squat

Figure 6–41 Vertical Leg Press

Vertical Leg Press

The vertical leg press is similar to the half squat in terms of movement mechanics. (See Figure 6–41.) It involves both the quadriceps and hamstrings muscles, and enables the use of relatively heavy weightloads. Unlike the half squat, this exercise does not stress the shoulders and back, and can be executed safely without the assistance of a spotter.

The exerciser places the feet on the lifting bar, and positions the hips directly beneath the feet. The knees and the hips should be flexed to at least 90 degrees. The exerciser pushes the lifting bar upward until the legs are fully extended, pauses momentarily, and slowly lowers the weightload back to the starting position.

It is advisable to place a padded incline board under the back to provide support for the hips and lower back area. If desired, this exercise can also be used to train the calf muscles. The exerciser simply extends the ankles as far as possible at the completion of each repetition.

Figure 6–42   Seated Leg Press

Seated Leg Press

There are a number of exercise machines that permit the exerciser to perform a leg press from a sitting position. (See Figure 6–42.) Although the leg action is similar to that in the vertical leg press, care must be taken to keep the hips firmly pressed against the seat throughout the exercise. Any attempt to incorporate the lower back muscles reduces the training effect on the quadriceps and the hamstrings, and may lead to lower back injury.

The exerciser sits on the seat and places the feet on the lifting levers. The seat should be adjusted so that the knees and hips are flexed to at least 90 degrees. The lifting levers are pressed forward until the legs are completely extended, then returned slowly to the starting position.

There is a tendency to use the seated leg press for demonstrating strength rather than developing strength. Because relatively heavy weightloads can be utilized in this exercise, it is important to perform slow, controlled movements to maximize the strength benefits and minimize the possibility of injury.

Dead Lift

The dead lift incorporates the quadriceps and hamstrings, along with the powerful lower back muscles. (See Figure 6–43.) As might be

Figure 6–43 Dead Lift

expected, this exercise permits the use of heavy weights, and must therefore be performed with strict attention to form. In simplest terms, the dead lift merely involves bringing a barbell from the floor to the upper thighs. However, one must be careful to maximize the role of the legs to prevent excessive stress on the lower back muscles.

The exerciser squats behind the barbell, and takes a mixed, shoulder-width grip on the bar. The first movement must be with the legs, not with the back. The barbell is lifted off the floor by extending the knees and the hips. Once the barbell is in motion, the back should begin to straighten. When the exerciser becomes erect, there is a momentary pause, then the barbell is returned to the floor. (This is one exercise in which the return movement is not done slowly!)

Because heavy weightloads are generally used when doing dead lifts, it is important to execute the movements in the proper sequence. The initial phase of the lift should involve only knee extension and hip extension, not back extension. The lowering movement should be the reverse of the lifting movement. Although the barbell should not be dropped to the floor, resistance to the downward movement is necessarily less pronounced in the dead lift than in most other exercises. Some people find it helpful to wear a lifting belt (for lower back support) when performing dead lifts.

Power Clean

The power clean is a dynamic exercise that can be performed with a relatively heavy barbell. (See Figures 6–44, 6–45, and 6–46.) It involves

153

Figure 6–44   Power Clean

Figure 6–45   Power Clean

Figure 6–46 Power Clean

the quadriceps, hamstrings, lower back, shoulders, trapezius, biceps, and calf muscles. Because the quadriceps and hamstrings muscles initiate the upward movement of the barbell, they play the major role in this exercise.

The exerciser begins by squatting behind the barbell and taking an overhand, shoulder-width grip on the bar. With the arms extended and the back straight, the exerciser lifts the barbell off the floor with forceful contraction of the quadriceps and hamstrings muscles. Once the barbell is in motion, there is a sequential activation of the lower back, trapezius, shoulder, biceps, and calf muscles. The bar is pulled upward in a straight line until the elbows are as high as possible. When the barbell reaches its highest point, the elbows are swung forward and the bar is caught in a shoulder rest position. After a brief pause, the barbell is returned to the floor. As in the dead lift, the barbell need not be lowered slowly, but should be under the exerciser's control.

The power clean is perhaps the most powerful and explosive exercise presented in this book. Although all exercises in which the weights are essentially thrown and caught present a greater risk of injury, power cleans are not dangerous when executed correctly. As long as the back remains straight and the legs provide most of the movement force, the probability of injury is minimized. The exerciser may find it advantageous to wear a lifting belt when performing power cleans.

Figure 6–47 Dumbbell Jump Squat

Dumbbell Jump Squat

Another explosive-type exercise for the quadriceps, hamstrings, and calf muscles is the dumbbell jump squat. (See Figure 6–47.) This is performed with relatively light weightloads, because the combined resistance (bodyweight and dumbbells) is moved over a large vertical distance.

The exerciser assumes a staggered (front-back) foot position, and holds the dumbbells at full arm's extension. The exerciser squats down until the knees are flexed about 90 degrees, then jumps upward with as much force as possible. Just prior to landing the feet are switched and the knees are flexed to absorb the downward force. There is no pause between successive repetitions.

The dumbbell jump squat is a convenient and effective exercise for strengthening the leg muscles. It is important, however, to flex the ankles, knees, and hips upon landing to dissipate the shock and reduce the chance of injury.

Leg Extension

The leg extension provides an excellent training stimulus for the quadriceps muscles. (See Figure 6–48.) Unlike the previously described

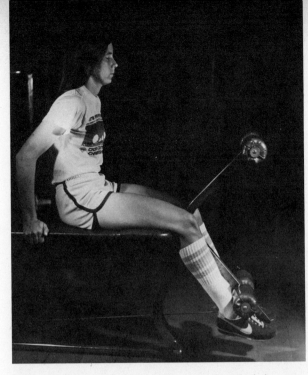

Figure 6–48 Leg Extension

leg exercises, the leg extension is a single joint movement that effectively isolates the quadriceps.

The first step in performing this exercise is to sit on the leg extension apparatus with the hands on the sides of the bench and the ankles underneath the padded lifting bar. The exerciser moves the lifting bar upward until the legs are fully extended. After a momentary pause, the lifting bar is slowly lowered back to the starting position. The back should remain straight through the exercise.

It is important to bring the legs to complete extension (lockout) on every repetition. Holding a heavy resistance in a near-lockout position places great stress on the knee joint. Consequently, if the lockout position cannot be achieved, the set should be terminated and/or the weightload should be reduced.

Leg Curl

One of the few exercises that deals specifically with the hamstrings muscles is the leg curl. (See Figure 6–49.) The leg curl and the leg extension complement each other and should be performed together to promote muscle balance between the quadriceps and the hamstrings groups.

The exerciser lies face down on the leg curl apparatus, grips the

157

Figure 6–49 Leg Curl

sides of the bench near the shoulders, and places the heels underneath the padded lifting bar. The lifting bar is curled toward the buttocks until the knees are flexed as far as possible. After a brief pause, the lifting bar is returned slowly to the starting position.

There is a tendency to lift the hips off the bench slightly during the performance of this exercise. While this is not a serious problem, pronounced hip movement is an indication that the weightload should be reduced.

Heel Raise

The standard exercise for developing the calf muscles is the heel raise. (See Figure 6–50.) This is a simple exercise that can be performed in a variety of ways.

Figure 6–50 Heel Raise

Perhaps the simplest way to execute the heel raise is to place a relatively heavy barbell across the shoulders, and lift the heels off the floor as far as possible. After a brief hold in the top position, lower the heels back to the floor.

It is recommended that a two-inch board be placed under the balls of the feet when performing this exercise. This enables a greater range of movement, and thereby increases the training effect on the calf muscles.

Toe Raise

Few people perform specific exercises for the shin muscles. It is important, however, to pair a shin muscle exercise with a calf muscle exercise in order to maintain muscle balance in the lower legs. The toe raise is an effective and easily performed exercise for the shin muscle group. (See Figure 6–51.)

The exerciser sits on a high bench or table, with the lower legs hanging over the side. A barbell plate is attached to a rope and suspended from the toes. The exerciser begins with the foot pointed downward. The toes are then lifted towards the shins as far as possible, held momentarily, and slowly returned to the starting position.

Toe raises can be performed with both feet simultaneously, but better control can be obtained when each leg is exercised individually. The lower leg should remain stationary throughout the exercise.

Figure 6–51 Toe Raise

EXERCISES FOR THE FOREARMS

The forearm muscles are involved to some degree in all exercises in which the bar is gripped with the hands. However, with a few exceptions (e.g., arm curls), the forearms are seldom stressed to the point of fatigue. It is therefore advisable to include some specific exercises for forearm development. These exercises involve wrist flexion (moving the palms towards the wrists) and wrist extension (moving the palms away from the wrists).

Wrist Curl

Wrist curls provide an excellent training stimulus for the forearm flexor muscles. (See Figure 6–52.) Because this is a very specific exercise, relatively light resistance is sufficient to fatigue the forearm flexors.

The exerciser sits on a bench or chair, with the forearms resting on the thighs and the wrists hanging over the knees. The exerciser takes an underhand grip on the barbell and curls it as high as possible without lifting the forearms off the thighs. After a brief pause in the top position, the barbell is slowly lowered as far as possible.

Although the range of movement is very limited, wrist curls provide a direct application of stress and quickly fatigue the forearm flexors when performed in a slow, controlled manner. Many people prefer to do wrist curls shortly after performing arm curls.

Figure 6–52 Wrist Curl

Figure 6–53   Wrist Extension

Wrist Extension

Wrist extensions are the reverse of wrist curls. (See Figure 6–53.) They are also characterized by a short range of movement and relatively light weightloads.

After assuming a sitting position on a bench or chair, the exerciser places the forearms on the thighs with the wrists hanging over the knees. The exerciser grasps the barbell with an overhand grip, and lifts it as high as possible without taking the forearms off the thighs. After a momentary hold in the top position, the barbell is slowly lowered as far as possible.

Like the wrist curl, this is a very effective exercise due to its directness. Wrist extensions isolate the forearm extensor muscles and provide sufficient training stimulus for strength augmentation.

Wrist Roll

The wrist roll is a versatile forearm exercise that can be directed to either the forearm flexor muscles or the forearm extensor muscles. (See Figure 6–54.) It is, perhaps, the most fatiguing of all the forearm exercises.

161

Figure 6–54 Wrist Roll

    The wrist roll apparatus consists of a barbell plate attached by a two-foot length of rope to a short piece of pipe. The exerciser extends the arms forward from the shoulders, takes an overhand grip on the pipe, and rotates it in the desired direction. When all of the rope is wrapped around the pipe, the exerciser reverses the direction of rotation and slowly lowers the weight. If the weight is lifted with clockwise pipe rotation, the wrist flexors provide the movement force. Conversely, if the weight is lifted by means of counterclockwise pipe rotation, the wrist extensors are the prime mover muscle group.

    The wrist roll is a rather unusual exercise, but it is very effective for developing the forearm muscles. Due to the number of pipe rotations necessary to hoist the weight, a relatively light barbell plate (five to ten pounds) is usually sufficient to provide the desired training effect. Although it is not necessary to hold the arms at shoulder height, better results seem to be obtained when this is done.

EXERCISES FOR THE MIDSECTION

The abdominal muscles and oblique muscles that flex and twist the trunk, respectively, are referred to as the midsection muscles. Although most midsection exercises involve hip flexion, this is not really a function of the midsection muscles. Hip flexion is actually performed by the quadriceps, and the underlying iliopsoas and pectineus muscles. Because traditional situps involve both trunk flexion and hip flexion, the abdominals are the prime mover muscle group for the first phase of the movement, but the hip flexors are responsible for the second phase of the movement. While there is nothing wrong with exercises that combine trunk flexion and hip flexion, specialized movements will be presented for those people who prefer to train the midsection muscles independently.

The midsection muscles respond to the Stress Adaptation Principle (see Chapter Three) in the same manner as other skeletal muscles. In other words, the resistance should be relatively high and the number of repetitions should be relatively low. The typical midsection workout of 100 to 200 situps at the end of each training session will not produce optimal strength development in the midsection muscles.

Bent Knee Situp

The standard exercise for the midsection muscles is the bent knee situp. (See Figure 6–55.) The bent knee situp is initiated by the abdomi-

Figure 6–55 Bent Knee Situp

nal muscles and completed by the hip flexor muscles (quadriceps, iliopsoas, and pectineus).

The exerciser assumes a back-lying position on the floor, with the knees bent and the hands folded behind the neck. The trunk is elevated to a vertical position (the elbows should contact the knees), then lowered slowly until the shoulders return to the floor.

When the feet are held down, the contribution of the hip flexor muscles is increased. When the feet are not secured to the floor, the activity of the abdominal muscles is enhanced. Due to body structure, most men need to have their feet secured, especially when holding a barbell plate behind their neck. For these individuals, bent knee situps tend to place greater emphasis on the hip flexor muscles than on the abdominal muscles.

Incline Situp

One way to increase the stress on the midsection muscles is to place more weight behind the neck. Another means of making the situp more difficult to perform is to use an incline board. (See Figure 6–56.) The steeper the incline, the harder the midsection muscles must work against gravity.

The exerciser lies on the incline board with the feet secured, knees bent, and hands folded behind the neck. The trunk is raised until the elbows touch the knees, then returned slowly back to the incline board.

Performing situps on an incline board places greater stress on both

Figure 6–56 Incline Situp

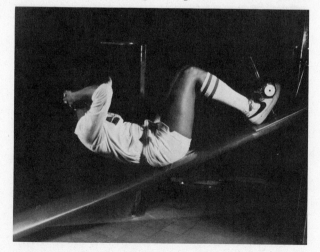

the abdominal muscles and hip flexor muscles. The intensity of the exercises can be increased by raising the incline board, adding more weight behind the neck, or both. The involvement of the oblique muscles can be maximized by twisting the trunk from side to side on alternate repetitions (i.e., right elbow to left knee, left elbow to right knee).

Roman Chair Situp

The Roman chair situp is another means for improving upon the basic situp. (See Figure 6–57.) This exercise involves both trunk flexion and hip flexion, and enables the prime mover muscles to contract over a greater range of movement. It also places the abdominals on stretch prior to the start of each repetition.

The Roman chair situp may be performed over a bench or on a specially designed apparatus. The exerciser sits across the bench, with the feet hooked under a barbell, and the hands folded behind the neck. The starting position is assumed by lowering the trunk toward the floor until the midsection muscles are comfortably stretched. The exerciser raises the trunk to a sitting position, then slowly returns to the starting position.

Roman chair situps enable the hip flexor and trunk flexor muscles to produce force over a greater distance than is possible with other midsection exercises. However, due to the hyperextension of the lower back in the down position, the exerciser must be careful to move slowly, and to stay within a comfortable range of movement.

Figure 6–57 Roman Chair Situp

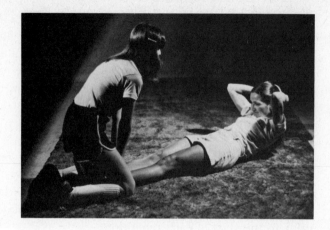

Figure 6–58   Abdominal Curl

Abdominal Curl

One exercise specifically designed for the midsection muscles is the abdominal curl. (See Figure 6–58.) Unlike other midsection exercises, abdominal curls involve trunk flexion but not hip flexion. Consequently, the abdominals are the prime mover muscle group for the entire curling movement.

Trunk curls are performed from a back-lying position, with the hands folded behind the neck. Because hip flexion is not a factor in this exercise, the legs may be straight or bent depending on personal preference. The exerciser curls the shoulders forward as far as possible, without lifting the lower back off the floor. After a momentary pause, the shoulders are slowly returned to the floor.

Abdominal curls may be described as an attempt to press the lower back into the floor. In the starting position, the upper back is on the floor and the lower back is off the floor. At the completion of the curling movement, the upper back is off the floor and the lower back is on the floor.

Although the shoulders are lifted only a few inches off the floor, this exercise produces an excellent training effect on the midsection muscles. Because the abdominals are tensed through the entire movement, relatively few repetitions of this exercise are necessary to fatigue this muscle group. Abdominal curls are also beneficial for the lower back area, because they round the lower back and stretch the lower back muscles.

Stress can be progressively increased by adding weight behind the neck, performing the exercises on an adjustable incline board, or both. The oblique muscles can be activated by twisting the trunk to the left and to the right on alternate repetitions.

Incline Knee-up

The incline knee-up is essentially an incline situp done in reverse. (See Figure 6–59.) Instead of securing the feet and lifting the trunk, the trunk is secured and the legs are lifted. Although incline knee-ups involve both hip flexion and trunk flexion, they are reasonably effective for strengthening both of these muscle groups.

The exerciser assumes a back-lying position with the hands secured to the top of the incline board. With the knees flexed, the legs are curled backward until the thighs almost touch the chest. The legs are then slowly lowered back down to the incline board.

This exercise provides a good range of movement, and allows for progression by means of an adjustable incline board, ankle weights, or both. One should be careful, however, to keep the knees bent throughout the exercise to reduce stress on the lower back area.

Figure 6–59 Incline Knee-up

Hanging Knee-up

Knee-ups can also be performed from a hanging position. (See Figure 6–60.) Hanging knee-ups are performed in direct opposition to

Figure 6–60 Hanging Knee-up

gravity, and are, therefore, somewhat more strenuous than those done on an incline board. They also tend to emphasize hip flexion to a greater degree than trunk flexion. This exercise is executed from a full-hang position on a pull-up bar. Without flexing the arms, the knees are bent and lifted toward the chest. After a brief pause in the top position, the legs are slowly lowered back down to a full hang.

Although hanging knee-ups can be performed with straight legs, this places greater stress on the lower back area. The resistance can be increased by wearing ankle weights or by attaching barbell plates to the feet. By alternately twisting the knees to the left side and right side, the oblique muscles can obtain a significant training effect from this exercise.

Jackknife Situp

The jackknife situp essentially combines a situp and a knee-up in a single exercise. (See Figure 6–61.) It is a dynamic movement that involves both trunk flexion and hip flexion.

The exerciser assumes a back-lying position with the knees straight and the arms at the sides. At the same time, the trunk is curled forward and the knees are flexed backward so that the exerciser is balanced on the buttocks with knees to the chest. After a brief pause, the trunk and legs are simultaneously returned to the starting position.

168

Figure 6–61 Jackknife Situp

Although balance and coordination play a major role in the execution of this exercise, it can produce a high level of tension in both the hip flexor and trunk flexor muscles. It is a challenging exercise that is often used to put the finishing touches on a midsection workout.

EXERCISES FOR THE LOWER BACK

One of the most critical areas in the human body is the lower back. If the lower back musculature becomes too weak or too tight, serious physical consequences can occur. Because the lower back muscles are responsible for back extension, and also for transmitting forces between the legs and trunk, it is important that these muscles be both strong and flexible. The following exercises are useful for strengthening the muscles of the lower back. They should be paired with appropriate back stretching exercises and midsection strengthening exercises to ensure flexibility and muscle balance throughout the waist area.

Back Hyperextension

One of the simplest and most effective exercises for strengthening the lower back is the back hyperextension. (See Figure 6–62.) This exercise is essentially a reverse abdominal curl.

Figure 6–62 Back Hyperextension

The exerciser lies face down on the floor, with the hands folded behind the neck. With a partner holding the feet on the floor, the exerciser lifts the head and shoulders as high as possible. After a brief pause, the head and shoulders are slowly lowered back to the floor.

Stress can be increased by adding resistance behind the neck, or by performing the exercise on a high table. In the latter case, the exercise begins with the torso off the table at a right angle to the legs. This enables the lower back muscles to produce force over a greater range of movement.

Stiff-legged Dead Lift

Unlike the standard dead lift, which is essentially a leg exercise, the stiff-legged dead lift is specifically designed to strengthen the lower back muscles. (See Figure 6–63.) Because the legs play a minor role in this exercise, relatively light weightloads must be used.

The exerciser begins by standing behind the barbell, bending at the waist, and grasping the bar with an overhand grip. Without bending the legs or the arms, the exerciser lifts the barbell to the upper thighs by straightening the back. After a momentary hold, the barbell is returned slowly to the floor.

Due to the leverage factors involved in the stiff-legged dead lift, the exerciser must use weightloads that permit slow and controlled movements. Any attempt to jerk the weight could be potentially harmful, and should be avoided.

Figure 6–63 Stiff-legged Dead Lift

Figure 6–64 Good Morning

Good Morning

The good morning exercise is similar to the stiff-legged dead lift in that the entire lifting force is produced by the lower back muscles. (See Figure 6–64.) Due to this factor and the rather precarious placement of the resistance, relatively light weightloads must be utilized in this exercise.

The exerciser begins by placing a barbell across the shoulders, and standing with the feet a little more than shoulder width apart. Without bending the legs, the exerciser leans forward until the back is approximately parallel to the floor. The back is then straightened so that the trunk assumes an erect position.

Although the legs remain straight throughout this exercise, the hips move slightly backward during the lowering phase, and slightly forward during the lifting phase to maintain balance. When performed in a slow and controlled manner, the good morning is an excellent exercise for strengthening the lower back muscles.

EXERCISES FOR UNIVERSAL GYM AND SIMILAR WEIGHT MACHINES

Weight machines like the Universal Gym provide a safe, convenient, and efficient way to train. The use of weight stacks eliminates the need to change barbell plates between exercise sets, and saves a considerable amount of time and energy. The proximity of the various exercise stations is another useful feature. Although the space requirement is minimal, several persons can train at the same time without interfering with each other. The design of the equipment also permits one to train without the assistance of a partner or spotter. Universal Gym machines have excellent safety and durability records.

The only feature on the Universal Gym that may cause difficulty is the fixed movement path established by the lifting levers. For some individuals, the movement pattern required by the machine places excessive stress on the joint structures. Any exercise that creates discomfort in the joint area should be immediately discontinued before serious tissue damage occurs.

Because each of the exercises recommended for Universal Gym training is discussed in the previous section on barbell training, only a brief description of each exercise will be presented in the following section.

Universal Bench Press

The exerciser lies on the bench so that the lifting lever is in line with the upper chest. (See Figure 6–65.) The lifting lever is pressed upward to full arm's extension, and lowered slowly to the starting position. The weights need not be returned all the way to the stack between repetitions if this places too much stretch on the chest and shoulder muscles. The head, shoulders, and buttocks should remain in contact with the bench throughout the exercise.

Figure 6–65 Universal Bench Press

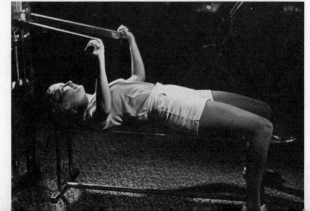

Figure 6-66   Universal Pull-down

Universal Pull-down

This exercise is performed by sitting or kneeling beneath the pulley, taking the preferred grip on the bar, and pulling it to the upper chest. (See Figure 6–66.) After a brief pause, the bar is slowly returned to full arm's extension. As the weightload approaches bodyweight, the feet must be secured to prevent the exerciser from being lifted off the floor.

Universal Seated Row

The exerciser assumes a sitting position in front of the pulley, takes the preferred grip on the bar, and pulls it to the chest. (See Figure 6–67.) After a momentary hold, the bar is returned slowly to full arm's extension. The back should remain in a vertical position throughout the exercise.

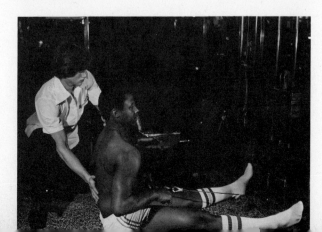

Figure 6-67   Universal Seated Row

Figure 6–68 Universal Pull-up—Narrow

Universal Pull-up

This exercise begins with a full body hang from the pull-up bar. (See Figure 6–68.) The exerciser pulls the chest to the bar, pauses momentarily, and returns slowly to the starting position. An underhand, shoulder-width grip is recommended. Resistance can be added by attaching barbell plates to the waist if desired.

Universal Standing Press

The Universal standing press is performed by placing the hands on the lifting lever and pressing it upward to full arm's extension. (See Figure 6–69.) After a brief pause in the lockout position, the lifting lever is slowly lowered to shoulder level. It is recommended that this exercise not be performed from a seated position, as this forces the shoulders to follow a fixed and inflexible movement pathway.

Figure 6–69 Universal Standing Press

Universal Upright Row

The exerciser stands in front of the pulley, and takes a narrow, overhand grip on the bar. (See Figure 6–70.) With the elbows leading the movement, the bar is pulled straight up to the chin, held momentarily, and returned slowly to full arm's extension. The back should remain straight throughout the exercise.

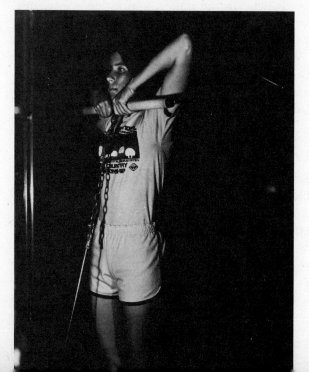

Figure 6–70 Universal Upright Row

Figure 6–71 Universal Press-down

Universal Press-down

The exerciser stands beneath the pulley, and assumes a narrow, overhand grip on the bar. (See Figure 6–71.) The elbows should be against the sides and the bar should be held at about neck level with the arms fully flexed. Without changing the position of the elbows, the bar is pressed downwards to full arm's extension, held briefly, and returned slowly to the starting position. The back should remain straight throughout the exercise.

Universal Bar Dip

This exercise begins from a support position on the dipping bars. (See Figure 6–72.) The exerciser lowers the body as far as possible between the bars, then presses back up to full arm's extension. This exercise should be performed slowly to avoid swinging. Resistance can be added if desired by attaching barbell plates to the waist.

Figure 6–72 Universal Bar Dip

Universal Curl

The exerciser stands in front of the pulley and takes an underhand grip on the bar. (See Figure 6–73.) The elbows should be against the sides, and the bar should be at full arm's extension across the upper thighs. Without changing the position on the elbows, the bar is curled to the neck, held momentarily, and lowered slowly to the starting position. The back should remain straight throughout the exercise.

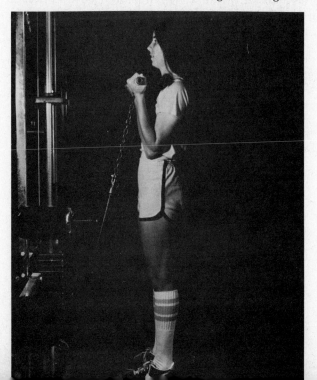

Figure 6–73 Universal Curl

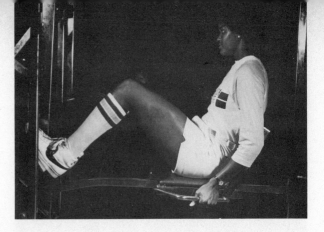

Figure 6-74   Universal Leg Press

Universal Leg Press

After assuming a seated position, the exerciser places the feet on the preferred lifting lever. (See Figure 6–74.) The lever is pressed forward until the legs are fully extended. After a brief pause, the legs are returned slowly to the starting position. The buttocks should remain in contact with the seat at all times during this exercise. Each repetition should terminate in the lockout position.

Universal Leg Extension

The exerciser sits on the leg extension apparatus with the ankles hooked under the padded lifting bar. (See Figure 6–75.) The bar is lifted upward until the legs are fully extended, held momentarily, and returned slowly to the starting position. There should be no attempt to lean backward during the lifting phase of the exercise. If the exerciser

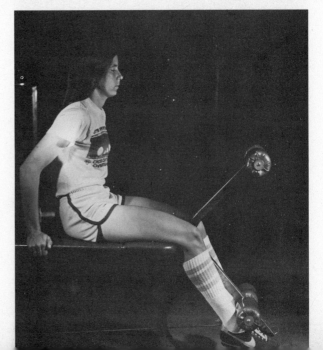

Figure 6-75   Universal Leg Extension

has difficulty reaching the lockout position, the weightload should be reduced.

Universal Leg Curl

The exerciser lies face down on the leg curl apparatus, grasps the sides of the bench near the shoulders, and places the feet under the padded lifting lever. (See Figure 6–76.) The lifting lever is pulled toward the buttocks until the knees are flexed as far as possible, held briefly, and slowly returned to the starting position. The hips should not be allowed to lift more than a few inches off the bench during the exercise.

Figure 6–76 Universal Leg Curl

Universal Incline Situp

The exerciser assumes a back-lying position on the incline board, with the knees bent and the hands folded behind the neck. (See Figure 6–77.) The trunk is raised to a sitting position (elbows touching knees),

Figure 6–77 Universal Incline Situp

then lowered slowly back to the incline board. The difficulty of this exercise can be increased by using a steeper incline, placing a barbell plate behind the neck, or both.

Universal Incline Leg Raise

The exerciser takes a back-lying position, with the hands secured to the top of the incline board. (See Figure 6–78.) The knees are pulled as close as possible to the chest, held momentarily, and returned slowly back to the incline board. The legs should be bent during most of the exercise to reduce stress on the lower back area.

Figure 6–78 Universal Incline Leg Raises

Universal Back Hyperextension

The Universal Gym offers a specially designed apparatus for performing back hyperextensions. (See Figure 6–79.) The exerciser places the hips on the padded seat, secures the feet to the anchor bar, and lets the trunk hang downward at a right angle to the legs. The trunk is elevated as high as possible, held momentarily, and returned slowly to the starting position. If greater resistance is desired, a barbell plate can be held behind the neck during the exercise.

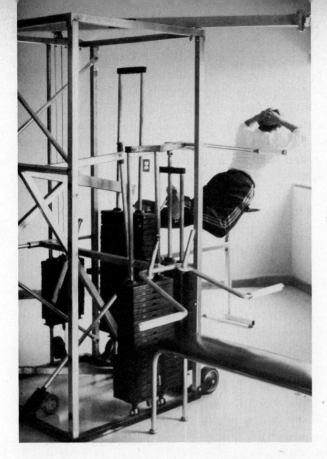

Figure 6–79 Universal Back Hyperextension

EXERCISES FOR NAUTILUS EQUIPMENT

The present day Nautilus exercise machines are the result of Arthur Jones' persistent efforts to develop a more efficient means of strength training. According to Ellington Darden, Nautilus Director of Research, Nautilus equipment features ten aspects of full-range exercise. These are: 1) rotary movement, 2) direct resistance, 3) automatically variable resistance, 4) balanced resistance, 5) positive work, 6) negative work, 7) stretching, 8) pre-stretching, 9) resistance in position of full contraction, and 10) unrestricted speed of movement.

As discussed in Chapter Five, exercise that provides for direct resistance, rotary movement, and automatically variable resistance may be more effective than conventional training. By applying the resistance directly to the target muscle group, opposing the resistance to the movement pathway, and accommodating the resistance to the strength curve, greater muscular stress can be realized.

Nautilus equipment is safe, durable, and carefully designed to give the exerciser control over the training session. Although training partners are recommended for a variety of reasons, they are not necessary for operating the machines or for obtaining a training effect. Nautilus machines can be adjusted to fit persons of various sizes and physiques. However, once positioned on the machine, the movement pathway is fixed and inflexible. The exerciser must, therefore, be careful to adjust each machine prior to its use, and to discontinue any exercise that produces discomfort in the joint area. The following exercises are recommended when the appropriate Nautilus machines are available.

Nautilus Hip and Back Extension

This exercise strengthens the hip extensors, buttocks, and lower back muscles. (See Figure 6–80.) It is performed on the Nautilus Super Hip and Back Machine. The exerciser assumes a back-lying position on the machine, with the shoulders against the shoulder pads, the hands on the grips, and the seat belt fastened. The hip joint should be in line with the machine axis of rotation, and the padded lifting lever should be across the back of the thighs. Beginning from a position of full hip flexion, the exerciser pushes the lifting lever forward until the hips are completely extended. After a brief pause, the legs are returned slowly to the starting position. It is important that every repetition be performed through a full range of movement.

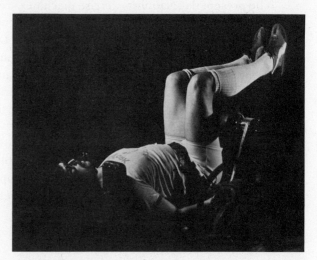

Figure 6–80 Nautilus Hip and Back Extension

Figure 6–81 Nautilus Leg Press

Nautilus Leg Press

The Nautilus Leg Press involves the quadriceps and hamstrings muscles, and is performed on the Leg Press Machine. (See Figure 6–81.) The exerciser places the feet on the lifting lever, and adjusts the seat position so that the knees are flexed at least 90 degrees. With the hands on the grips, and the buttocks on the seat, the lifting lever is pressed forward until the legs are fully extended. Following a brief pause, the legs are slowly returned to the starting position. The leg press should not stop short of full extension (lockout position), as this may place excessive stress on the knee joint.

Nautilus Leg Extension

This exercise is performed on the Leg Extension Machine, and effectively isolates the quadriceps muscles. (See Figure 6–82.) The exer-

Figure 6–82 Nautilus Leg Extension

ciser sits on the bench, grips the handles, and places the ankles under the padded lifting lever. The lifting lever is raised until the legs are fully extended, held momentarily, and slowly lowered back to the starting position. The back should remain straight throughout the exercise, and each repetition should terminate in the lockout position.

Nautilus Leg Curl

The Nautilus leg curl is a specialized exercise for the hamstring muscles that is done on the Leg Curl Machine. (See Figure 6–83.) After assuming a front-lying position on the bench, the exerciser grips the handles, and places the heels under the padded lifting lever. The lifting lever is pulled towards the buttocks until the legs are fully flexed, then returned slowly to the starting position. The hips should not lift more than a couple of inches off the table during the execution of this exercise.

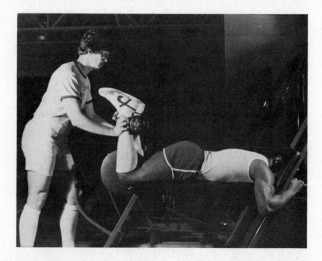

Figure 6–83   Nautilus Leg Curl

Nautilus Pull-over and Pull-down

These exercises are usually performed in combination on the Nautilus Pull-over/Pull-down Machine. (See Figures 6–84 and 6–85.) The pull-over isolates the latissimus dorsi, and is done first to fatigue this muscle group. The pull-down, which incorporates both the lats and the biceps, is then executed without delay to fully exhaust the latissimus muscles. This procedure is generally referred to as the pre-exhaustion method of stressing a target muscle group.

The exerciser positions the seat so that the tops of the shoulders are in line with the machine's axis of rotation. The seat belt is secured, the lifting lever is moved into the starting position, and the elbows are placed on the lifting pads. The lifting lever is forced downward by the elbows until the extension bar touches the waist. The elbows are then raised slowly until the latissimus muscles are in a fully stretched position. The head and upper back should remain in contact with the seat back throughout the exercise.

Immediately following a set of pull-overs, the exerciser disengages the elbows, and grasps the pull-down bar with an underhand grip. The bar is pulled to the upper chest, held momentarily, and returned slowly to full arm's extension. In this exercise, as in the pull-over, the exerciser should concentrate on bringing the elbows down to the sides.

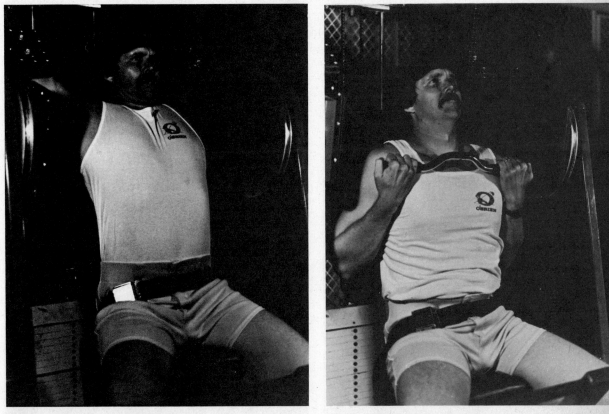

Figure 6–84 Nautilus Pull-over

Figure 6–85 Nautilus Pull-down

Nautilus Lateral Raise and Seated Press

These exercises are usually done together on the Nautilus Double Shoulder Machine. (See Figures 6–86 and 6–87.) In accordance with the pre-exhaustion procedure, the lateral raise is performed first because it isolates the deltoid muscles. The seated press, which utilizes both the deltoids and the triceps, follows immediately to further stress the shoulder muscles.

The lateral raise is performed by aligning the shoulders with the machine's axes of rotation, fastening the seat belt, and placing the back of the hands against the lifting pads. With the elbows leading the movement, the lifting levers are raised until the arms are parallel to the floor. After a brief pause, the elbows are slowly lowered back to the sides.

As soon as the final lateral raise has been completed the exerciser adjusts the weightload and grasps the lifting lever for the seated press exercise. The lifting lever is pressed upward to full arm's extension, held momentarily, and lowered slowly to the shoulders. The head and upper back should remain in contact with the seat back throughout both of these exercises.

Figure 6–86   Nautilus Lateral Raise

Figure 6–87   Nautilus Seated Press

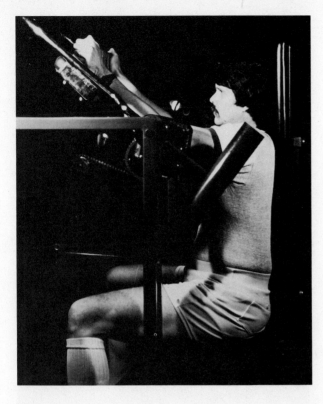

Figure 6–88 Nautilus Triceps Extension

Nautilus Triceps Extension

This exercise effectively isolates the triceps muscles, and is performed on the Nautilus Biceps/Triceps Machine. (See Figure 6–88.) The exerciser assumes a seated position, and rests the elbows on the stabilizer pad, in line with the machine's axis of rotation. The wrists are placed on the lifting pads, and the lower arms are rotated backward to a position of full elbow flexion. Without taking the elbows off the stabilizer pad, the lifting lever is pushed forward until the arms are fully extended. After a short pause, the lifting lever is returned slowly back to the starting position.

Nautilus Biceps Curl

The biceps curl is the complement to the triceps extension, and is also performed on the Nautilus Biceps/Triceps Machine. (See Figure

Figure 6-89   Nautilus Biceps Curl

6–89.) The exerciser sits on the bench, places the elbows on the stabilizer pad in line with the machine's axis of rotation, and takes an underhand grip on the lifting lever. Beginning from full arm's extension, the lifting lever is curled upward as far as possible. Following a brief hold, the lifting lever is slowly lowered to the starting position. The torso should remain in a fixed position throughout the exercise to prevent the use of assisting body movements, and to place maximum stress on the biceps muscle.

Nautilus Shoulder Shrug

This exercise, performed on the Nautilus Shoulder Shrug Machine, is specifically designed to isolate the upper trapezius muscles. (See Figure 6–90.) The exerciser sits on the bench and places the forearms, palms upwards, between the lifting pads. With no attempt to involve the arm muscles, the shoulder girdle is raised as high as possible, held momen-

Figure 6–90 Nautilus Shoulder Shrug

tarily, and lowered slowly to the starting position. The head and torso should be held erect throughout the exercise. Also, arm flexion is less likely to occur when the biceps remain in contact with the back of the lifting pads.

Nautilus Seated Row

The seated row utilizes the upper back and posterior shoulder muscles, and is executed on the Nautilus Seated Row Machine. (See Figure 6–91.) The exerciser assumes a seated position with the back firmly against the back rest. The elbows are placed on the lifting pads, and the upper arms are rotated forward until the shoulders are comfortably stretched. The lifting levers are pushed backward as far as possible, held momentarily, and returned slowly to the starting position. The arms should remain parallel to the floor throughout the exercise.

Figure 6–91 Nautilus Seated Row

Nautilus Bent Arm Fly and Decline Press

These exercises are usually executed consecutively on the Nautilus Double Chest Machine. (See Figures 6–92 and 6–93.) Because the bent arm fly effectively isolates the chest muscles, it is performed first. The

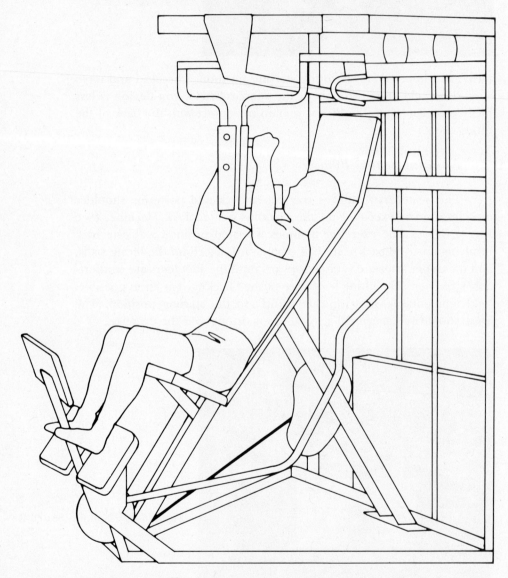

Figure 6–92 Nautilus Bent Arm Fly

decline press, which involves the triceps and anterior deltoids as well as the pectoralis, is done immediately afterward to completely fatigue the chest muscles.

The exerciser sits on the decline bench and secures the seat belt. The forearms are placed against the lifting pads, and the handgrips

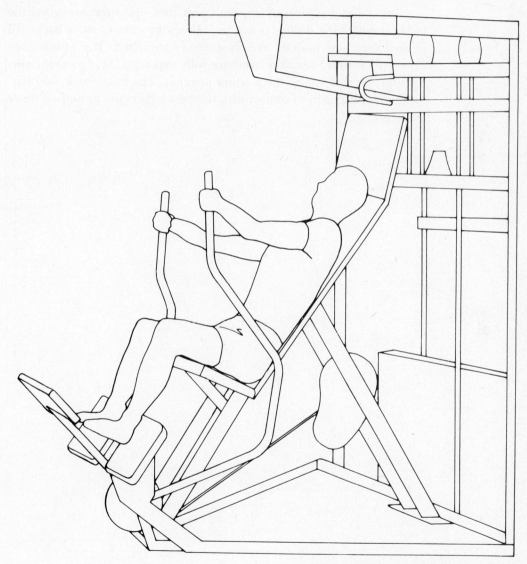

Figure 6–93 Nautilus Decline Press

are held loosely. The bent arm fly begins with the elbows back far enough to place a stretch on the chest muscles. The arms are then rotated forward until the lever pads come together in front of the face. After a momentary hold, the arms are returned slowly to the starting position. One should concentrate on squeezing the elbows together during the concentric phase of this exercise.

At the completion of the bent arm flies, the exerciser grips the lifting lever for the decline press, and allows the arms to move backward so that the chest muscles are comfortably stretched. The lifting lever is pressed forward until the arms are fully extended, held momentarily, then returned slowly to the starting position. The head, back, and buttocks should remain in contact with the bench throughout both of these exercises.

Chapter Seven

Facts about Strength Training

The development of strength fitness is a complex phenomenon that involves numerous physiological adaptations to imposed training stimuli. When people effectively incorporate the Principles of Stress Adaptation, Rebuilding Time, Near-Maximum Resistance, Controlled Movement Speed, Full-Range Movement, Muscle Balance, and Training Specificity (see Chapter Three, Principles of Strength Training), they are almost certain to produce positive physiological adaptations and experience increases in muscular strength. However, it is impossible to predict the rate at which any given individual will gain muscle strength or size. The relationship between strength training and strength improvement is relatively stable over time, but it is rather unpredictable on a day-to-day or even a week-to-week basis.

Table 7–1 presents the rates of strength gain over successive 2½-week training periods for three different training groups. Group A made the greatest increment in strength during the first 2½-week training

Table 7–1   Rates of Strength Gain over Successive Two-and-One-Half Week Training Periods for Three Different Training Groups

Training Group	n	Avg. Str. Inc. during First 2½ Weeks of Training	Avg. Str. Inc. during Second 2½ Weeks of Training	Avg. Str. Inc. during Third 2½ Weeks of Training
A	13	10.6%	6.1%	5.4%
B	20	5.5%	5.7%	4.6%
C	16	6.4%	4.0%	7.2%

period. In fact, the rate of strength gain for this group was almost twice as high during the first training period as during the second and third training periods. Group B, on the other hand, experienced a relatively even rate of strength development, with the greatest increase occurring during the second 2½-week training period. The response from Group C was also different from that of the other groups. This group achieved a relatively high rate of strength gain during the first training period, a relatively low rate of strength gain during the second training period, and the greatest improvement in strength during the third 2½-week training period. The rates of strength development for individuals within each of these groups was even more variable, further demonstrating that one's physiological response to strength training is difficult to predict.

Generally speaking, as one continues to train, greater stimulus is required to produce further strength gains. That is, more training stress is necessary to maintain one's muscular progress. A problem arises, however, when greater and greater amounts of stress result in smaller and smaller increments in strength. This state of affairs, often referred to as staleness, is common to athletes in all fitness-related activities. Distance runners and weightlifters are alike in that improvement comes more quickly during the first months of practice and less easily as they get closer to their maximum performance potential. For example, a weightlifter who increases his bench press by five pounds a week at the start of his program may improve less than five pounds a year after several years of training, even though the training intensity is considerably greater.

Although it would be nice if everyone's rate of strength gain resembled that displayed in Figure 7–1, a more accurate and realistic representation of strength development is presented in Figure 7–2. As indicated in the latter figure, the rate of strength gain decreases throughout the duration of one's training career, and eventually becomes a rate of strength decrement due to the aging process. The non-training individual begins to lose strength around age 25, but the person who trains can build strength for many more years, and can postpone the loss of strength that inevitably accompanies middle age.

Basically, the principle of diminishing returns applies to the process of strength development. At first, brief workouts result in relatively large strength gains, whereas, later, long workouts produce relatively small increments in strength. For years, weightlifters have rebelled against diminishing rates of strength development by doubling and tripling the

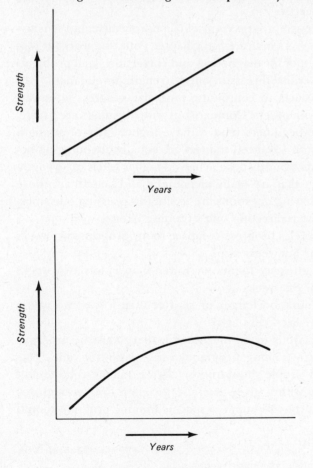

Figure 7–1 Hypothetical relationship between strength development and years of training. In this example, the rate of strength gain remains constant throughout the duration of the training program.

Figure 7–2 Hypothetical relationship between strength development and years of training. In this example, the rate of strength gain decreases throughout the duration of the training program, and eventually becomes a rate of strength loss.

length of their training sessions. It is doubtful that this practice significantly increases their rate of strength gain. Unfortunately, extensive workout sessions have often had the opposite effect. At best, too much stress prevents positive strength adaptations from taking place. At worst, it results in chronically fatigued muscles, strength decrement, and tissue injury.

Well-informed exercisers realize that strength gains are simply going to come more slowly as training continues. They do not fight this natural phenomenon, but simply train in harmony with it. They do not expend two or three times the amount of energy necessary to achieve optimal progress, but they do increase the intensity of the training program. As Darden (1977) has so aptly stated: "An advanced trainee does not need more exercise than a beginner; he needs harder exercise and in most cases less exercise."[1]

The key to continued progress is gradual improvement and sensitivity to stumbling blocks. As indicated in Chapter Four, the workout logbook is an invaluable tool for diagnosing and correcting small problems before they become serious threats to one's strength development. Perhaps the greatest obstacle to continuing muscular progress is unwarranted comparisons with others. Comparisons with beginners are usually discouraging because beginners tend to have higher rates of strength gains. Comparisons with advanced trainers are equally discouraging because these individuals typically have achieved higher levels of strength. The only comparisons that are really meaningful and helpful are those with oneself. The following questions are useful for assessing one's personal progress and for redirecting one's training efforts:

How does this week's progress compare to my progress two weeks ago? Four weeks ago? Six weeks ago?

Is my workout intensity higher or lower than it was two weeks ago? Four weeks ago? Six weeks ago?

Is my workout duration longer or shorter than it was two weeks ago? Four weeks ago? Six weeks ago?

For such comparisons to be meaningful, there must be a degree of consistency in one's training program over a period of time. This is not to suggest that people should never alter a training routine, but that they should stay with a given exercise program long enough for it to be effective. As a rule of thumb, a specific training program should

---

1. Ellington Darden, *Strength Training Principles: How to Get the Most Out of Your Workouts.* (Winter Park, Florida: Anna Publishing, Inc., 1977), p. 38.

be given a six-week trial period to fairly assess its effect on strength development.

There are basically four training variables involved in the performance of a particular exercise.

Resistance: As the resistance or weightload is increased, the muscular stress is likewise increased. Generally speaking, the use of a relatively heavy resistance (i.e., a weightload that cannot be lifted more than 10 to 12 times in a row) is the most critical factor in promoting strength development.

Repetitions: Up to a point, as the number of repetitions performed with a given weightload is increased, the muscular stress is also increased. However, when more than 10 to 12 repetitions can be completed, the resistance is no longer sufficient to produce optimal gains in strength, and should be increased.

Sets: Much like repetitions, increasing the number of sets performed increases the cumulative amount of muscular stress. However, when the resistance is relatively heavy, only a few sets can be completed due to the muscle fatigue that results from high intensity exercise.

Recovery Time: As the recovery time between sets of exercises is decreased, the muscular stress is, in effect, increased. That is, the shorter the rest interval between sets, the more difficult it is for the muscles to accommodate the training resistance.

Taking these four training variables into account, one means for providing a degree of standardization in one's training program is to establish a fixed weightload, a fixed number of sets, and a fixed recovery time. That leaves the number of repetitions as the only training variable to be dealt with during any given workout. This enables one to easily evaluate personal progress over a period of time. Consider the following example:

Example

Joan decided to begin a weight training program to increase the strength of her quadriceps muscles. Her basic training exercise was leg extensions. During her first workout, she performed three sets of leg extensions with 60 pounds. She rested two minutes between sets, and executed 10, 8, and 7 repetitions respectively, for a total of 25 repetitions. To objectively assess her progress in this exercise, Joan followed the same workout pattern for six weeks, training three times per week. Whenever she completed 10 repetitions for all three sets of leg extensions, she increased the weightload by 5 pounds and again began the process of adding repetitions.

This procedure actually represents what is known as a double progressive training system. The primary variable is the number of repetitions, because during any given training session the weightload, number of sets, and rest interval remain fixed. The secondary variable is the resistance, because whenever three sets of 10 repetitions are achieved the weightload is increased slightly. In other words, Joan first strives to perform three sets of 10 repetitions with a particular weightload. When she attains this objective, more weight is added and she works toward three sets of 10 repetitions with the new weightload.

When Joan looks over her workout logbook she finds that six weeks ago she did 25 repetitions (10-8-7) with 60 pounds. Four weeks ago she performed 28 repetitions (10-9-9) with 70 pounds. Two weeks ago she executed 30 repetitions (10-10-10) with 80 pounds. Today she completed 27 repetitions (10-9-8) with 85 pounds.

Joan has obviously made progress and should continue her training program for at least a few more weeks. If, on the other hand, Joan had experienced little or no strength improvement over a six-week training period, then she should definitely change her workout routine.

───────────────────────────────

The important point to remember is that rational decisions regarding one's training program can best be made when one utilizes a systematic and progressive approach to strength development. Changing the exercises, weightloads, sets, repetitions, and rest periods from workout to workout makes program evaluation difficult. Continued progress is dependent upon the identification and incorporation of those training procedures that seem to be most effective for promoting strength gains. People who train on a day-to-day basis are less likely to discover an optimal training program and more likely to become discouraged with their workouts than people who are consistent and persistent in their approach to strength development.

STRENGTH PLATEAUS

When one's progress comes to a halt, one is said to be experiencing a strength plateau. This is sometimes referred to as peaking out, but most strength enthusiasts believe that they can further increase their strength once the cause of the problem is resolved. For the most part, this assumption is correct. The difficulty is in identifying and rectifying the cause of the problem.

It is generally agreed that a strength plateau is an indication that some aspect of the training program should be changed. Such a change would usually involve one or more of the following training variables: exercise selection, exercise sequence, weightload, number of repetitions, number of sets, length of rest intervals, and training frequency. Other considerations may include the type of exercise equipment utilized, the type of diet one is following, and whether to train alone or with a partner.

Although there are numerous factors involved, the basic decision is whether to make one's workout more demanding or less demanding. It has been the author's experience that persons on a strength plateau invariably choose to work harder in an attempt to force further strength development. In most cases, this strategy either maintains the plateau level of strength or results in strength loss. Doing more of the same activity that led to the strength plateau seldom initiates new strength gains. The better alternative is to reduce one's workout demands temporarily to allow the muscle recovery and rebuilding processes to catch up. Remember that positive muscle adaptations occur during the rest period following the training session. Consequently, the first thing one should do to get off a strength plateau is to schedule more recovery time between workouts. Some seasoned weightlifters have found that taking an entire week off from training is the most effective means of improving their performance.

As indicated in the previous paragraphs, strength plateaus often result when too little recovery time is taken between strenuous workouts, preventing the muscles from rebuilding to higher levels of strength. (See Chapter Three, Principle of Rebuilding Time.) If extended recovery periods do not improve the situation, the exerciser should seriously consider changing the workout routine.

The first alteration of the established training program should deal with the exercise intensity. For example, if one has been training with three sets of ten repetitions, one could increase the weightload and perform three sets of five repetitions. It may very well be that the muscles have become so accustomed to the 10RM weightload that this training stimulus no longer promotes positive strength adaptations. Conversely, persons who have been working with three sets of five repetitions could reduce the weightload and execute more repetitions per set. Although higher resistance is usually more conducive to strength development, it is sometimes necessary to do more repetitions with a lighter weightload in order to attain the desired muscle response.

The author has found it helpful to switch training programs completely upon encountering a strength plateau. For example, if one is utilizing the DeLorme-Watkins training system (a 10RM system), it may be beneficial to change to the Berger program (a 6RM system) or the pyramid program (a 1RM system). These training programs are presented in detail in Chapter Four.

If a change in workout intensity does not stimulate further strength gains, it may be necessary to select different training exercises. Many competitive powerlifters have discovered that the best way to get off of a strength plateau in the bench press is to temporarily eliminate this exercise from their training routine. They simply substitute another chest-shoulder-triceps exercise, such as a decline press, an incline press, or a dumbbell bench press. After a period of training with the substitute exercise, they return to the bench press and frequently surpass their plateau level strength after a few workouts.

As indicated in Chapter Six, there are several exercises that can be performed for each of the major muscle groups. Also, any barbell exercise can be effectively executed with dumbbells. The benefit of changing exercises is apparently related to the use of different fibers within a particular muscle group. Different exercises tend to stress different parts of the muscle, which seems to enhance the overall strength of the muscle. If increased recovery time and different workout intensities have little effect on one's strength plateau, a change of exercises may be in order.

Sometimes, nothing seems to have an impact on a stagnated strength level. A friend of the author, at the time a nationally ranked super-heavyweight powerlifter, encountered this problem. One could have assumed that he had reached his maximum potential in the three power lifts, but he did not do this. Instead, he cut his training program from six days a week to three days a week, and began jogging on his non-lifting days. It was not too long before he bettered each of his personal lifting records, and his strength improved well beyond the levels at which he had previously plateaued.

Did the running cause the improvement in strength? Perhaps not directly, but it may have contributed in several indirect ways. To begin with, powerlifters do not obtain much in the way of continuous activity from their workouts. They typically perform a few repetitions with a relatively heavy weightload, and then rest several minutes before performing another set. A three-hour training session may therefore involve less than ten minutes of actual physical activity. This type of training does not produce any positive physiological adaptations of the heart or circulatory system. Consequently, the increase in muscle mass developed through weight training is not paralleled by an increase in the ability of the cardiovascular system to supply blood to these muscles.

The efficient delivery of oxygen and nutrients to and the effective removal of carbon dioxide and metabolic wastes from the working muscle cells are dependent upon the condition of the heart and cardiovascular system. It is, therefore, important to develop a cardiovascular system that is capable of meeting the needs of larger and stronger muscles, particularly during the recovery period immediately following an exercise bout.

When a fisher buys a larger boat, she or he also buys a larger engine to power the boat. In like manner, the person who builds larger muscles should also perform some activity to strengthen the cardiovascular system. Running, cycling, rope jumping, and swimming are excellent supplementary activities for persons who train with weights. Such activities do not directly improve one's muscle size or strength, but they do promote cardiovascular efficiency which may facilitate one's physiological adaptations to high intensity muscle training.

The time and effort required to improve cardiovascular health are not great, and the benefits to one's personal health and feeling of well-being are clearly worth the investment. Details on how to effectively train the cardiovascular system are given later in this chapter.

Strength plateaus appear to be an inevitable consequence of continued training. Regardless of the training program utilized, there seems to come a time when a change of one type or another is necessary to stimulate further strength development. Strength plateaus should not be cause for discouragement. They are simply reminders that it is time to revise the training routine. It may be an indication for more rest, higher intensity training, alternate exercises, supplementary exercises, or complementary types of activity. Whatever change may be necessary, it should be viewed as a positive step toward one's optimal muscular development.

PROTEIN AND MUSCLE BUILDING

The questions most frequently asked by strength training enthusiasts are undoubtedly those related to diet, particularly the type and amount of protein that should be injested for optimal muscular development. These are important questions, because proteins are directly responsible for the increased size and strength of trained muscle fibers. In addition to the actin and myosin proteins that form the structural and functional units of skeletal muscle, creatine protein is vital to the process of muscle contraction. Protein is also essential for the formation of bone tissue, blood, and the hormones that influence various physiological processes.

While few people question the importance of protein in the diet, there is considerable disagreement over the amount of protein one should consume on a daily basis, particularly when engaged in heavy strength training activities. The recommended daily protein requirement for adults is one gram of protein for every kilogram (2.2 pounds) of body weight. That is, an adult who weighs 90 kilograms (198 pounds) should obtain about 90 grams of protein, which is equivalent to 3.2 ounces of protein. Most Americans consume this much protein in the course of a day simply by following a normal, well-balanced diet. Persons who wish to increase their protein intake can easily do so by eating more protein-rich foods such as milk, cheese, yogurt, eggs, fish, chicken, beef, peanuts, soybeans, and nuts. There are also a variety of protein pills, powders, and liquids commercially available. These are legitimate products which provide an excellent source of extra protein.

The fact is, however, that extra protein generally is not utilized by the body. Neither marathon runners nor weight trainers require additional protein if their daily diet is basically sound. This is true even for persons who are involved in heavy strength training and muscle building activities. It appears that the anabolic (tissue building) processes of the body occur at a relatively constant rate, and are not significantly accelerated by the presence of additional protein. Therefore, optimal muscular development may be obtained without protein supplements, if one adheres to sound nutritional guidelines.

Although there are numerous recommendations concerning training diets and nutritional supplements, there is no research evidence that a good basic diet can be improved upon in terms of enhancing one's muscular development. Such a diet generally contains all of the proteins, carbohydrates, fats, vitamins, and minerals necessary for optimal health. There are four basic categories of foods that should be included in one's daily meals.

Category 1—Meat-Poultry-Fish-Protein Foods

It is recommended that one obtain at least two servings per day of foods with a high protein content, such as the following:

Beans	Nuts
Beef (lean)	Peanuts/Peanut Butter
Chicken	Pork (lean)
Eggs	Soybeans
Fish	Turkey
Lamb	Wild Game
Liver	

Although it is not necessary to eat meat to meet one's daily protein requirements, it is important to obtain all of the amino acids that are essential for protein synthesis. There are at least ten essential amino acids that cannot be manufactured in the human body, and which must be included in the diet. Meat, eggs, and milk products supply all of these essential amino acids, but no single vegetable, fruit, grain, or nut does so.

Because proteins obtained from animal sources contain all of the amino acids essential for tissue building and repair, they are often referred to as complete or high-quality proteins. Conversely, proteins derived from other food sources do not provide all of the essential amino acids, and are therefore called incomplete or low-quality proteins. It is possible for vegetarians to obtain all of the essential amino acids even though they do not consume meat or dairy products. They must, however, be knowledgeable about the types of proteins contained in their foods, and be certain to eat a variety of vegetables, fruits, grains, and nuts to ensure that none of the essential amino acids are excluded from their diet.

Category 2—Dairy Products

In addition to the protein sources discussed in Category 1, it is recommended that one obtain two or more servings of dairy products on a daily basis. Dairy products are excellent sources of high-quality proteins, and include the following:

Cottage Cheese	Skim Milk
Ice Cream/Ice Milk	Whole Milk
Natural Cheese	Yogurt

There has been considerable disagreement regarding the advantages and disadvantages of consuming dairy products when training for muscular strength and definition. The major point of controversy is over the relatively high fat content of whole milk products. Because skim milk and other low-fat dairy products are readily available in nearly all grocery stores, there does not seem to be any good reason, other than allergic reactions, to avoid this highly nutritious food source. Skim milk furnishes the same amount of protein and calcium as whole milk, but has less saturated fat and fewer calories. It is interesting to note that the principal ingredient in most commercially prepared high-protein supplements (powders, pills, and liquids) is non-fat dried milk.

Category 3—Fruit and Vegetables

Fruit and vegetables should make up a large percentage of one's daily food intake. It is recommended that at least four servings in this group be consumed each day. All sorts of fruits and vegetables are included in this category, including citrus fruit, apples, peaches, pears, berries, dried fruit, bananas, melons, lettuce, tomatoes, carrots, peppers, onions, potatoes, peas, beans, greens, squash, corn, broccoli, cauliflower, asparagus, cabbage, celery, and beets.

Although most fruit and vegetables do not have a high protein content, they are generally excellent sources for carbohydrates, and for the various vitamins and minerals that are necessary for optimal physical health and athletic performance.

Category 4—Cereals and Grains

Many Americans derive too many calories from this food group. Nonetheless, it is recommended that one obtain at least four servings per day from these food sources. Because it includes breads, pasta, and baked goods, this category is typically the one that people partake of the most. Consider the following food items that are made from cereals and grains:

Biscuits	Oat Cereals
Breads	Pancakes
Cakes	Pies
Cobblers	Rice
Cookies	Rice Cereals
Corn Cereals	Rolls
Crackers	Spaghetti
Doughnuts	Waffles
Macaroni	Wheat Cereals
Natural Cereals	Wheat Germ
Noodles	

Obviously, the foods in this category vary greatly in nutritional and caloric value. Basically, those that are highly refined and comprised largely of white flour, white sugar, and shortening are lower in nutritional value and higher in calories. Examples include cakes, cobblers, cookies, doughnuts, and pies. On the other hand, whole grain products such as dark breads, natural cereals, brown rice, and wheat germ have greater nutritional value and fewer calories. Other grain-based foods such as cereals, crackers, macaroni, and spaghetti fall somewhere in between depending on the grain source utilized. Many grains and cereals have the additional advantage of providing fiber that is so important to the efficient functioning of the digestive system.

The person who eats a balanced diet (one which approximates the recommended number of servings from the four basic food groups) should obtain sufficient protein, as well as the necessary vitamins and minerals, to enable maximum gains in muscle size and strength. In other words, protein supplementation is not necessary for promoting muscular gains. On the other hand, although excessive amounts of protein can place a burden on the kidneys, a moderate increase in one's protein consumption is not physically harmful, and may be psychologically helpful to an athlete involved in heavy training. The author can think of few better ways to supplement one's diet, as long as a healthy balance among the four major food groups is maintained. Undoubtedly, a can of tuna fish and a glass of skimmed milk provides a more nutritious lunch than a bag of potato chips, a candy bar, and a soft drink.

Finally, it is interesting to note that almost all serious bodybuilders and weight trainers consume considerably more protein than is recommended. In fact, most physique contestants try to maintain a daily protein intake of 1.5 to 2.0 grams per kilogram of bodyweight. Although supporting research evidence is not currently available, it may be that persons involved in intense weight training programs respond more favorably (particularly with respect to muscle hypertrophy) when larger amounts of protein are ingested.

Sample Diet for Bodybuilders

As indicated earlier in this section, proteins are composed of various combinations of amino acids. Because there are ten essential and ten nonessential amino acids, some protein foods are of more value than others in tissue building and repair. The best proteins for supplying human growth and maintenance needs are those from animal sources, such as eggs, meat, fish, poultry, and milk products. However, because heavy consumption of meats appears to have a relatively high correlation with heart disease and certain types of cancer, it is recommended that several protein sources be utilized in the bodybuilder's diet.

Actually, meat ranks only sixth, behind eggs, milk, fish, cheese, and whole grain rice in terms of protein quality. Other excellent sources of high quality protein include oats, rye, wheat germ, wheat flour, soy flour, peas, beans, potatoes, sweet potatoes, and spinach. Various nuts, peanuts, and peanut butter are also useful protein sources.

Of course, bodybuilders need foods from all of the basic food groups to meet their overall nutritional requirements. However, they typically ingest as little fat as possible to reduce subcutaneous fat deposits and enhance muscle definition.

With this in mind, a bodybuilder's breakfast might consist of soft boiled eggs on whole wheat bread, wheat germ with raisins and low-fat milk, low-fat yogurt, and orange juice. For lunch, tuna fish packed in water, tossed salad with a tablespoon of oil and vinegar, low-fat cheese, low-fat milk, an apple, and an orange should suffice. The evening meal could include broiled fish with lemon, whole grain rice, sweet potatoes, peas, rye bread without butter, fresh fruit salad, vegetable juice, low-fat milk, and walnut stuffed dates. Appropriate snack foods would be peanuts, peanut butter, low-fat yogurt, low-fat cheese, low-fat milk, fresh fruit, or a mixture of rolled oats, raisins, dates, and assorted nutmeats.

The sample menu is presented simply as a guideline for obtaining good nutrition while emphasizing protein consumption and restricting fat intake. It should go without saying that chicken, turkey, or veal could be substituted for fish and that a wide variety of fruit, vegetables, whole grains, and low-fat dairy products could be interchanged without disrupting the basic concept of the bodybuilder's diet.

MUSCLE AND FAT

There has been a widespread misunderstanding regarding the relationship between muscle and fat, particularly with respect to weight training. It is often said that the muscle one develops during the training period will turn to fat once the program is discontinued. This sometimes appears to be the case, but actually cannot happen. Muscle is a tissue that tends to get larger when it is used (hypertrophy) and smaller when it is not used (atrophy). Fat is a substance that accumulates in various parts of the body when one's caloric intake exceeds one's energy expenditure. Muscle cannot physically become fat or vice versa.

What frequently happens is this. A person begins a strength training program and experiences muscle hypertrophy. During the training period, caloric intake is increased to meet the new energy and tissue building requirements of the body. Because the energy demand is equal to the energy supply, fat is not deposited and the exerciser displays a well-defined, muscular physique. Then, for some reason, the strength training program is discontinued, and the muscles begin to decrease in size (atrophy). If the caloric intake is not correspondingly reduced to equal the lower energy requirements, fat will begin to accumulate. Consequently, the muscle may be replaced by fat as a result of stopping the exercise program but maintaining the same eating behavior. This phenomenon can be easily avoided by adjusting one's diet to the level of activity or inactivity. When this is done, the individual who stops working out will experience a gradual loss of muscle size and body weight, but will not become fat.

Another misconception concerning weight training is that the training process inevitably makes one bulky. The truth is that many weightlifters are bulky to begin with, not because they train with weights. For example, a stocky boy or girl may find little success in sports requiring speed, endurance, or agility, and may turn to weight training as an alternative activity. The weight training will increase muscle size and strength, but will not, by itself, eliminate a bulky appearance. Only a proper combination of diet and vigorous exercise can produce such a slimming effect. Consequently, one should not assume that a bulky weightlifter looks that way because of the strength training program. More than likely, he or she retains that appearance in spite of the strength training program.

It should be understood that one's basic body build cannot be substantially changed by a weight training program. There is no evidence that strength training can alter skeletal structure or increase the length of one's muscle bellies. Even the degree to which one gains muscle strength and size is, in part, genetically determined and regulated through hormone production.

In other words, strength training is limited in application to the muscles being exercised. One can bulk up by lifting weights and over-eating, and one can slim down by lifting weights and under-eating, but large changes in body weight are more likely the result of eating patterns than strength training programs.

If one is concerned with both losing fat and building muscle, then a more comprehensive training program should be undertaken. For example, running is more efficient than weight training for reducing body fat, while weight training is the most effective means for increasing muscle mass. Consequently, the person who is both soft and overweight could benefit most from a two-pronged training program. Running and weight training on alternate days is an excellent approach to overall conditioning, since the running improves one's endurance fitness and the weight training increases one's strength fitness.

STRENGTH AND FLEXIBILITY

Another important component of overall physical fitness, along with strength and endurance, is flexibility. The range of motion in a joint is a measure of flexibility, and has an important bearing on injury prevention and force production. Although the ideal range of motion about a joint has not been determined, a restricted movement range increases the likelihood of tissue injury when performing dynamic exercise.

With respect to athletic performance, the greater the distance over which an object is accelerated, the greater the force produced. Consequently, a discus thrower who increases shoulder girdle flexibility and utilizes a greater range of movement will throw further if all other factors (e.g., strength, technique) remain the same.

The key to joint flexibility is muscle stretchability, and the key to muscle stretchability is muscle relaxation. Muscle relaxation is the opposite of muscle contraction, and represents the absence of tension in the muscle fibers. Just as one must train the muscles to contract more forcefully, one must also train the muscles to relax more completely.

Muscles possess a property referred to as elasticity. That is, they return to their normal resting length after being stretched. If the stretch on a muscle is sudden, specialized control mechanisms called muscle spindles initiate a stretch reflex that results in a rapid and forceful muscle contraction. This is a protective reaction to prevent the muscle from being damaged by an abrupt or uncontrolled stretching force. For this reason, stretching exercises that involve rapid movements or bouncing are counterproductive, and not recommended for improving joint flexibility.

The best way to increase muscle stretchability is to perform slow, almost static, stretching movements. The muscle should first be stretched to a position of mild discomfort, then held in that position for a period of 20 to 30 seconds. During this time tension in the muscle should be released, the fibers should adjust to their new length, and the uncomfortable feeling should disappear. The muscle should then be stretched a little further until a slight feeling of discomfort is again experienced. Once more, this position should be maintained for about 20 to 30 seconds while the fibers adapt to their new length. This procedure should be performed a third time, then the muscle should be allowed to return to its normal resting length.

Effective muscle stretching is a slow process that must be carefully controlled for best results. Although muscles can certainly be stretched (and overstretched) through weight training, it is not recommended that one attempt to attain joint flexibility in this manner. A separate exercise program specifically designed to improve muscle stretchability is far more productive and less likely to cause tissue damage.

Although weight training does not usually produce greater flexibility, it has advantages over other types of exercise with respect to maintaining muscle balance and preventing muscle shortening. In most physical activities, (e.g., running, bicycling) the prime mover muscle groups eventually become stronger and shorter than their antagonists. This not only results in muscle imbalance and decreased joint mobility, but often leads to tissue injury.

There is no need for this to happen in a well-designed weight training program, because the prime mover muscle group in one exercise becomes the antagonist in the next exercise, and vice versa. For example, if one trains exclusively with bench presses, the chest and anterior shoulder muscles eventually become stronger and shorter while the back and posterior shoulder muscles become relatively weaker and longer. This leads to the round shouldered appearance observed in persons who do not include back exercises along with their chest work. However, the person who pairs an appropriate back exercise with each chest exercise will usually develop a balanced shoulder girdle musculature. Neither muscle group will become shorter because it is kept in check by a strong antagonist group.

Weight training will not reduce joint flexibility, as long as all the major muscle groups are included in the training routine. However, weight training is not the most effective way to enhance muscle stretchability and should not be substituted for a comprehensive program of stretching exercises.

It should be clear at this point that muscle strength and muscle flexibility are two separate things. The former represents a muscle's ability to contract, and the latter represents a muscle's ability to relax. Neither ability has a great influence on the other. A high level of strength does not preclude a high level of flexibility, or vice versa. The person who trains for both strength and flexibility is likely to achieve desired results in both of these fitness parameters.

Due to the all-out nature of strength training exercises, it is important for the antagonist muscles to relax completely while the prime movers lift the imposed weightload. This process, referred to as *reciprocal innervation,* eliminates internal resistance from other muscle groups, so that the available muscle force can be directed against the external resistance. Although research evidence is currently lacking, it is conceivable that regular strength training may enhance one's ability to reduce tension in antagonist muscle groups during heavy resistance exercise.

TRAINING EFFECTS IN WOMEN

The average adult female is approximately 3 to 4 inches shorter and 25 to 30 pounds lighter than the average adult male. In addition, she has about 10 to 15 pounds more fat and 40 to 45 pounds less fat-free weight (i.e., bone, muscle, organs). It is therefore not surprising that most females are weaker than their male counterparts. Indeed, strength studies with college age subjects reveal that males generally handle more than twice as much weight as females in the bench press exercise.

However, the rate of strength gain is similar for both males and females following any given training program. According to research findings by Westcott, college age men and women increase strength in the bench press exercise by approximately 3 to 4 percent per week. This indicates that the strength response to weight training is the same for women as for men. There is a difference, however, in the size response to weight training. Women do not typically experience the pronounced increases in lean body weight and muscle size that men achieve through a weight training program. The reason muscle hypertrophy is less prevalent in women appears to be related to the lower level of testosterone in women.

Because muscle strength is closely related to the muscle's cross-sectional area, and because women do not experience the increase in muscle mass that men do, women do not attain the same strength levels as men. This does not imply that all women are weaker than all men. To be sure, the strong female is likely to lift heavier weightloads than the untrained male. However, the strong female is not really close to the performance level of the strong male. This is true even when comparisons are made in terms of body weight.

For example, weightlifting competitions often utilize a strength quotient as a means of comparing the performance of various individuals. The simplest means of determining a person's pound for pound strength is to divide the amount of weight lifted by the bodyweight of the contestant. If a 150 pound male succeeded in bench pressing 250 pounds, his strength quotient would be 1.67 for that particular exercise (250 lbs $\div$ 150 lbs = 1.67). It is interesting to note that in most bench press contests the winning strength quotient for the men is close to 2.0, while the highest strength quotient for the women is approximately 1.0 to

1.4. When these figures are expressed in terms of lean body weight there is less difference, indicating that the male's greater muscle mass is largely responsible for his greater muscle strength.

It appears that women and men are similar with respect to the rate of strength development, but different in terms of the level of strength development. The limiting factor in female strength development seems to be muscle size. Due to lower levels of the male sex hormone testosterone, females do not typically experience significant increases in muscle mass and hypertrophy as a result of heavy resistance training. Women can, however, realize large increases in muscle strength, which is, after all, the most important outcome of a strength training program.

A recent study by Westcott has indicated that the effects of strength training may vary in females of different ages. Although further research is necessary, it would appear that young girls (ages 8–13) and teenage girls (ages 13 to 19) gain strength more rapidly than women over the age of 20. (Refer to Chapter Two, Age Factors.) Consequently, women should not be discouraged if their younger sisters seem to respond more favorably than themselves to a particular program of strength training.

The important point is that women can improve their muscular strength through a progressive system of weight training. The only training response difference between males and females is the degree to which muscle strength and hypertrophy are developed. The strength training principles and procedures are identical for men and women, and the same basic exercise program can be followed by all persons, regardless of sex or age.

TRAINING EFFECTS AFTER THIRTY

The person who does not engage in a systematic program of strength building activities experiences a gradual decrease in muscular strength some time during the late twenties and early thirties. The rate of strength loss becomes greater during the succeeding decades, and is, of course, a natural part of the aging process. Although research evidence is lacking, there have been enough individual examples to indicate that high strength levels can be maintained throughout the thirties, forties, and fifties. It also appears evident that the rate of strength loss can be reduced. Furthermore, with the exception of the person who has continued to train during adulthood, one's current strength level can be increased regardless of age. That is, adults who begin a strength training program will experience gains in muscular strength whether they are 35 or 65.

As a hypothetical example, let's assume that Mr. Jones was an avid weightlifter during his college years, and at that time was capable of bench pressing 300 pounds. After graduation he discontinued his training program and has done nothing more strenuous than lawn work and recreational sports for the past 20 years. Now, at 40 years of age, he decides to engage in serious strength training once again. He finds that, although he is about 15 pounds heavier than his college weight, he can now bench press only 160 pounds. After four months of training he is able to bench press 220 pounds, and after one year he is up to 270 pounds. Further training maintains but does not increase his strength level. In comparison to his college best, Mr. Jones is only 90 percent $\left(\dfrac{270 \text{ lbs.}}{300 \text{ lbs.}}\right)$ as strong at 41 years of age as he was at age 20. However, he is 170 percent $\left(\dfrac{270 \text{ lbs.}}{160 \text{ lbs.}}\right)$ stronger at 41 years of age than he was at 40.

Although a few weightlifters and bodybuilders are still competitive in their forties, the real challenge for most of us is to be the best we can be at the present time. The phenomenal growth of jogging and distance running has in large part been due to the emphasis on self-improvement and a higher level of personal endurance fitness. There is no reason the same motivation should not apply to weight training and strength development. Strength fitness is an important component of physical fitness, and should be a desired goal for men and women of all ages.

Critics of strength training often claim that muscular strength is not necessary in today's automated society. That may be true, but then neither is the ability to run 15 miles. The point is that both strength fitness and endurance fitness are worthy goals because they add quality to life. Furthermore, most people who exercise on a regular basis find the training process enjoyable, and feel better after a session of vigorous muscular activity.

Weight training has been accused of causing damage to the heart and circulatory system due to its strenuous nature. Although strength training does not promote cardiovascular health the way running and other endurance activities do, it is not harmful to a healthy individual of any age when performed properly. Proper execution includes two basic safety factors: 1) inhaling and exhaling with every repetition and 2) keeping the weight moving throughout every repetition. Holding the breath or holding the weight in a given position for more than a moment occludes blood flow and quickly elevates the blood pressure. While these guidelines should be followed by all exercisers, they are a must for persons over 30 years of age and for persons who have coronary risk factors.

The best way to avoid breath holding and prolonged straining with a weight is to use a resistance that can be lifted about ten times. Whenever the exerciser reaches a sticking point, the set should be terminated and the weight immediately lowered. Straining to complete a final repetition or holding the weight in an isometric contraction is not necessary for strength development, and is a potentially dangerous procedure for persons with circulatory problems.

With respect to overexertion, weight training may be compared to snow shoveling. Persons who work within their capacity, lifting small loads of snow, should not experience any difficulty in clearing the driveway. On the other hand, persons who struggle to carry as much snow as possible every time they lift the shovel are likely to be headed for trouble. Any all-out effort that produces an isometric or near-isometric contraction should be avoided whenever possible by persons over age 30.

It is for this very reason that weight training is an excellent strength building activity for persons of all ages. No matter how weak a person may be, the weightload can always be adjusted so that ten repetitions can be completed with moderate effort. This is not always the case for other strength related activities, particularly calisthenic exercises (e.g., pushups, pull-ups, dips) in which only one or two repetitions can be performed.

It is recommended that persons over 30 follow a general training program with exercises for each of the major muscle groups. In addition to observing the basic training principles and procedures, they should conscientiously avoid isometric contractions. The moment the weight stops moving, the set should be terminated. Persons over 30 should never struggle to squeeze out a final repetition. The strength benefits obtained from an additional repetition are too small to justify the risk of possible cardiovascular problems.

Finally, persons over 30 are encouraged to take a total approach to developing and maintaining physical fitness. Some form of endurance activity (e.g., running, swimming, bicycling) should be included to promote cardiovascular conditioning, strength training should be performed to ensure a reasonable level of muscular strength, and stretching exercises should be done to facilitate joint flexibility. Although the adult who has not been physically active should have a medical check-up before beginning a vigorous exercise program, it has been said that a medical examination is perhaps more necessary for the adult who chooses to remain sedentary.

WARM UPS

There has been considerable controversy over the advantages, disadvantages, or neutrality of performing warm-up exercises prior to athletic events and strenuous exercise sessions. Those in favor of using warm ups generally believe that the resulting increase in body temperature enhances the physical performance that follows. Those not in favor of warming up counter that increased body temperature is one of the factors that limits athletic performance, particularly in endurance type activities. In either case, it is interesting to note that most warm-up routines have a very insignificant effect on muscle temperature.

With regard to muscle stretchability, most people can temporarily increase their range of movement after performing stretching exercises. Some people prefer to stretch prior to doing the activity, while others feel that stretching is more useful and/or necessary immediately following activity. If range of movement is an important factor in the performance of the activity, then perhaps the appropriate stretching exercises should be done at the start of the activity.

Activities that require precise movement patterns seem to benefit from prior rehearsal in the form of progressively more forceful trials. For example, baseball pitchers, football quarterbacks, and shot putters invariably warm up with a few easy throws, then gradually increase the intensity until they are throwing at full effort. While this procedure seems to help groove the desired response pattern for movements that require fine motor control, its effect on the performance of gross motor movements, such as most weight training exercises, is not known.

Most weightlifters perform progressively heavier sets in some exercises (e.g., bench press, squat, dead lift), but not in others (e.g., curl, press-down, upright row). It is noted that warm-up lifts are more likely to be utilized in the exercises that incorporate relatively heavy resistance. While this may be physiologically beneficial in preparing the muscles for progressively heavier weightloads, it more likely serves as a psychological aid for building the exerciser's confidence prior to the big lifts. Whichever the case may be, the use of warm ups does not appear to hinder weight training performance, and is regarded by most lifters as a helpful procedure.

The warm-up program prior to a weight training workout should probably include some stretching exercises to ensure joint flexibility. Keep in mind that most weight training exercises have little effect on muscle stretchability, so the warm-up session could provide an excellent opportunity to deal with this fitness parameter. If the workout is going to include dynamic exercises, such as power cleans, specific stretching exercises and some lightweight practice lifts should be done during the warm-up period. Some people like to elevate their heart rate before beginning the training session. Jumping jacks, rope skipping, and various calisthenic exercises serve this purpose well, as does a five to ten minute jog.

If the exercise sets consist of ten repetitions, it is probably not necessary to perform warm-up sets with lighter weights. Under normal circumstances, a weightload that can be lifted ten times should not cause injury or require special preparation. On the other hand, if one is going to do single lifts with maximum poundages, it is recommended that a couple of progressively heavier warm-up sets be performed.

Perhaps just as important as the warm up is the cool-down period that follows the workout. Because weight training is a high intensity activity, large amounts of energy must be supplied to the muscles during contraction. Assuming that most exercise sets take between 30 and 60 seconds, part of this energy is supplied through anaerobic glycolysis and produces a fatigue by-product known as lactic acid. The longer the lactic acid remains in the muscles, the longer the recovery and re-building process takes. Because lactic acid is removed from the muscles by the blood, what one does immediately following the training period appears to affect the rate of lactic acid removal.

The person who goes directly from the weight room to the showers and then relaxes the rest of the day does little to expedite the recovery process. The person who immediately follows the workout with a big meal diverts the blood from the muscles to the digestive area and likewise fails to facilitate lactic acid removal. The person who runs a few sprints, does some vigorous rope jumping, or plays a hard game of handball to complete the workout produces more lactic acid and actually prolongs the recovery process. However, the person who does 15 to 20 minutes of moderate activity after the workout is likely to experience a faster recovery. The increased circulation that results from walking, jogging, easy swimming, or bicycling seems to hasten the rate of lactic acid removal. Once this fatigue compound has been eliminated from the muscles, the rebuilding process can proceed without interference.

To be most effective, the cool-down activity should not be merely an extension of the workout, but should involve several minutes of continuous rhythmical activity. The intensity of the cool-down activity should be high enough to produce moderate, but not heavy, breathing. Most of all it should be enjoyable, something to look forward to at the completion of the workout. A relaxed 15 minute swim is not only a pleasant way to end a training session, but can also increase joint flexibility and facilitate the removal of lactic acid from the muscles. The cool down can mean the difference between leaving the locker room feeling exhausted or feeling invigorated.

WEIGHT TRAINING FOR IMPROVED SPEED AND POWER

Speed is an important factor, perhaps the single most essential element, for successful performance in many athletic activities. Most sports participants would like to increase their speed of movement (running speed, throwing speed, striking speed, kicking speed, etc.) to enhance their performance level. Unfortunately, as every track coach knows, it is not easy to improve one's movement speed.

Speed is a complex neuromuscular phenomenon. Basically speaking, some people have it and some people do not. Although speed can be improved, no one really knows the best means for doing so. It is generally agreed that speed is most likely to be developed through repeated practice efforts. According to physiologists, repetition of a sports skill increases the probability that the more efficient nerve pathways will become grooved, and that the less efficient nerve pathways will be avoided.

There is actually little relation between speed of movement and strength of movement. That is, one can be strong but not fast, or fast but not strong. Although it is possible, and desirable, to be both strong and fast, one cannot train for speed and strength simultaneously. In fact, speed training is just the opposite of strength training. It is recalled that the key to strength development is intensity. High intensity training requires heavy resistance, and heavy resistance prohibits fast movements.

As an experiment, take a very light barbell and do a curl. Now take a heavy barbell, about the highest resistance you can curl once, and again perform a curl. You will not need a watch to convince you that the second lift was considerably slower than the first one. With the possible exception of throwing the weights, which is both a dangerous and non-productive procedure, high intensity training must be done slowly.

Speed training, on the other hand, must be performed as quickly as possible to produce the desired results. Because added resistance automatically slows movement time, weight training is not an appropriate means for developing movement speed. For example, let us say that a soccer player wants to increase the speed of his instep kick. He decides to do quick repetitions with 20 pounds in the leg extension exercise to enhance the explosive power of his kicking action. However, kicking a 20-pound resistance is quite different, and much slower, than kicking a soccer ball. Consequently, this type of training is not useful for improving kicking speed. Because the 20-pound resistance is of too low intensity to provide any strength benefits, there is little likelihood of producing greater explosive power. In other words, there is little benefit in performing rapid repetitions with light weights. Such exercises use too much resistance for improving speed and too little resistance for increasing strength, and are essentially useless for enhancing athletic performance.

As a second example, consider the shot putter who wants to deliver the shot more quickly. Can fast, lightweight incline presses produce a faster arm action in the shot put? Not unless the weight of the barbell (or dumbbell) is less than the weight of the shot (i.e., 16 pounds). In fact, even if the resistance were less than 16 pounds, the exercise would probably not improve the speed of the putting action because the movement patterns are quite different.

How, then, should one go about developing more speed in the shot put? Certainly not by practicing with a heavier implement, such as a 20-pound shot. In fact, just the opposite approach should be taken. Practicing with a lighter implement (e.g., 12-pound shot) will permit a faster arm action, which may eventually result in a speedier delivery with the 16-pound shot. The key to improving movement speed is repeated practice using the actual implement (shot, bat, racquet, etc.), or a slightly lighter implement. The use of weight training or heavier than regulation implements is not recommended for developing greater movement speed.

Muscle Power

Speed is quite often equated to power, but speed is only one component of power. Muscle power is actually dependent upon the interaction of three factors, speed, distance, and strength. An increase in the speed of contraction, distance of contraction, or strength of contraction will produce a corresponding increase in power.

In more scientific terms, power is the rate at which work is performed. That is, the amount of work performed during a given period of time is expressed in units of power. The power equation may be written as:

$$\text{Power} = \frac{\text{Work}}{\text{Time}}$$

Because work is technically defined as the application of force through a distance, power may also be expressed as the product of force and distance divided by time. This is represented as:

$$\text{Power} = \frac{\text{Force} \times \text{Distance}}{\text{Time}}$$

In accordance with this formula, one may increase power by increasing the movement force, increasing the distance over which the force is applied, or performing the movement in less time.

Although there are several technique-related factors that affect force application (see Appendix B), two physiological factors are basic to the production of muscular force. One is to increase the contractile strength of the muscle fibers, and the other is to increase the number of muscle fibers actively involved in contraction. Both of these physiological responses can be improved through strength training.

Persons with average speed, average range of movement, and

average strength can probably realize the greatest increase in power by developing their muscular force. Although speed training and flexibility training should not be neglected, the potential for greatest improvement typically lies with strength training. As indicated by research studies, strength gains of 4 to 6 percent per week can result from a systematic program of weight training. Even though the rate of strength gain decreases as higher strength levels are obtained, it is not unusual to increase strength by 30 to 35 percent over a two month training period.

Strength training for improved power should not take the form of fast repetitions with light weightloads. This type of training involves muscle exertion but does not produce the desired strength adaptations, because the resistance is too low. (See Chapter Three, Principle of Near-Maximum Resistance.) Keep in mind that there is a direct relationship between muscle force and power. The most effective way to develop muscle force is through a planned program of strength training that incorporates all of the basic strength training principles.

WEIGHT TRAINING FOR IMPROVED CARDIOVASCULAR AND MUSCULAR ENDURANCE

There has been considerable controversy over the endurance benefits associated with weight training. Unquestionably, a weight training program that promotes both cardiovascular and muscular endurance can be developed. However, it is doubtful that such a program would produce maximum strength improvement, because the requirements for strength fitness and endurance fitness are quite different.

It is recalled that strength is developed by high intensity training, which is necessarily of short duration. Just the opposite type of training is required to improve endurance. As implied by its name, endurance training demands a relatively long period of continuous exertion, which necessarily limits the intensity of the activity. Extensive research in the area of cardiovascular conditioning has revealed the following guidelines for obtaining endurance-related physiological adaptations:

Intensity: The activity must be vigorous enough to raise the heart rate of approximately 70 percent of maximum. Maximum heart rate varies with age, but can be predicted reasonably well by subtracting one's age from 220. Thus, the predicted maximum heart rate for a 40-year-old man is 180 beats per minute. He would therefore need to exercise at an intensity sufficient to elevate his heart rate to about 126 beats per minute (180 b/m $\times$ .70 = 126 b/m) to improve his cardiovascular endurance.

Duration: The activity must be of a continuous nature so that the heart rate will be maintained at the 70 percent of maximum level for 15 to 20 minutes or longer.

Frequency: The activity must be performed on a regular basis. Three non-consecutive days per week is usually considered the minimum training frequency for obtaining endurance-related benefits.

It is obvious that some activities do not conform well to these guidelines. Weight training, for example, is capable of temporarily elevating the heart rate beyond 70 percent of maximum, but it is not a continuous activity as usually practiced. In order to maintain the appropriate heart rate level over a 20-minute strength training session, one must either use relatively light resistance or follow a circuit training approach. The use of light resistance eliminates any strength-related benefits, and the circuit training approach is a compromise measure at best with regard to strength development.

Circuit training prevents resting between successive exercise bouts by moving immediately from an exercise for one body part (e.g., chest) to an exercise for a different body part (e.g., back), and so on until each major muscle group has been worked. The circuit may then be repeated in its entirety. Although circuit training undoubtedly offers some advantages over conventional training, the cumulative effects of fatigue force a reduction in weightload, which in turn reduces the stimulus for strength development.

Although any activity that elevates the heart rate to 70 percent of maximum, keeps it at that level for 20 minutes, and is performed at least three non-consecutive days per week will produce endurance-related physiological changes in the heart, blood vessels, blood, and muscles, some activities are particularly well-suited for achieving this objective. (See Appendix C for a description of the physiological adaptations to endurance exercise.) Large muscle, rhythmic activities such as jogging, bicycling, and swimming are highly recommended for developing both cardiovascular and muscular endurance.

The person who desires strength fitness and endurance fitness is advised to perform both strength exercises and endurance exercises. Keep in mind that strength training does not typically promote endurance fitness, endurance training does not promote strength fitness, and compromise programs such as circuit training seldom produce high levels of fitness in either area. The Principle of Training Specificity (i.e., strength training for strength fitness, endurance training for endurance fitness) must be observed to ensure optimal development in any fitness parameter. (See Chapter Three.)

An efficient way to improve both strength fitness and endurance fitness is through an alternate day training program. A 30 to 45 minute weight training workout on Monday, Wednesday, and Friday, and a 30 to 45 minute endurance activity (e.g., running, swimming, bicycling) on Tuesday, Thursday, and Saturday should provide sufficient opportunity to attain relatively high levels of strength fitness and endurance fitness over a period of three to six months. Such a program not only provides appropriate stimuli for the desired fitness results, but also permits the variety that makes the training program interesting and enjoyable.

WEIGHT TRAINING FOR IMPROVED SPORTS PERFORMANCE

There are a number of reasons people train with weights, and one of the foremost among these is the desire to improve sports performance. As indicated in a previous section, more strength means more power, and greater power means greater success in most athletic events. Over the past several years, coaches have learned that weight training can increase muscle size and strength without reducing speed and flexibility. Most athletic coaches, therefore, include some form of strength training in their sports programs. Athletes involved in team sports (e.g., football, soccer, basketball, volleyball, baseball, softball, lacrosse, hockey, European handball), dual sports (e.g., tennis, badminton, racquetball, handball, wrestling), and individual sports (e.g., track and field, cross-country, swimming and diving, gymnastics, bicycling, canoeing, golf, archery) can all benefit from well-designed weight training programs.

Persons interested in specific strength training exercises for a particular sport are referred to Stone and Kroll's book, *Sports Conditioning and Weight Training.* Regardless of the special requirements for a given athletic skill, there are certain guidelines that should be observed in any strength training program. To begin with, the program should include basic exercises for the major muscle groups. Exercises such as the bench press (chest, shoulders, triceps), pull-down (back, shoulders, biceps), and vertical leg press (quadriceps, hamstrings) are fundamental for developing strength in the large muscle groups of the body. Paired exercises for the arms (e.g., biceps curls and triceps press-downs) and legs (e.g., leg curls and leg extensions) are always beneficial, and promote the balanced muscle development that is so important for athletic success and injury prevention.

Actually, any of the exercises described in Chapter Six of this book are appropriate for athletes, as long as the overall program is consistent with the training principles presented in Chapter Three. It should be understood, however, that the main purpose of strength training exercises is to increase muscle strength. Therefore, exercises should be selected on the basis that they produce strength gains in the desired muscle groups. Exercises should not be included in a strength training program simply because they can be done explosively, or because they simulate a particular athletic skill. As indicated in a previous section, fast repetitions performed with light weights are not useful for improving either strength or speed.

Simulating a movement skill with a weight or other type of resistance is definitely not recommended for improving athletic performance. Although many outstanding athletes do exercises of this type, they are probably successful in spite of, rather than because of, this training procedure.

Perhaps the most widespread example of simulated resistance training is swinging a weighted bat. At best, practicing with a weighted bat is a highly inefficient means to increase strength in the contributing muscle groups. At worst, it is a potentially dangerous procedure that could lead to tissue injury. In any case, the slower movement speed experienced when swinging the heavier implement is likely to interfere with the precision timing required when swinging a regulation bat at a 93 mph fastball.

Another common example of simulated resistance training is the use of cables and other devices to imitate various throwing movements (e.g., baseball, football, javelin, discus, shot). There are several problems with this type of training. First, the simulated movement is usually just close enough to the actual skill pattern to confuse the neuromuscular response. Second, the added resistance always results in slower movement speeds. Third, the added resistance is usually insufficient to produce significant gains in strength. Fourth, performing throwing movements with heavier implements or with tethered resistance can place considerable stress on the shoulder, elbow, and wrist joints, and may cause injury.

The better approach for improving sports skills is to do strength training for increased muscle power, and technique training for better speed and coordination. To be successful, today's athlete must have a high level of strength and a high degree of movement skill. Both abilities are necessary for top athletic performance, and each is best developed through separate and specialized training programs. Every athlete can benefit from a sound program of strength development and a higher level of strength fitness.

Appendix A

Strength Training Equipment

Further information regarding barbells, dumbbells, Mini-Gym, Universal Gym, and Nautilus strength training equipment can be obtained by contacting the following addresses:

Mini-Gym
P.O. Box 266
Independence, Missouri 64051

Universal Gym
Nissen-Universal
P.O. Box 1270
Cedar Rapids, Iowa 52406

Nautilus Sports/Medical Industries
P.O. Box 1783
DeLand, Florida 32720

York Barbell Company
P.O. Box 1707
York, Pennsylvania 17405

Weider Barbell Company
21100 Erwin Street
Woodland Hills, California 91367

Appendix B

Principles of Force Production

There are certain basic principles of movement that should be observed when attempting to impart force to an object. The following principles of force production should be understood and applied by athletes involved in dynamic sports events.

Production of Force: To apply maximum force to an object, engage the maximum number of contributing muscle groups.

Direction of Force: To apply maximum force to an object, direct the force through the center of mass of the body and of the object.

Summation of Force: To apply maximum force to an object, begin each successive force at the height of the previous force.

Transfer of Weight: To apply maximum force to an object, move the center of mass in the direction of the force.

Range of Movement: To apply maximum force to an object, accelerate the object over the maximum possible distance.

Speed of Movement: To apply maximum force to an object, accelerate the object in the shortest possible time.

Action-Reaction: To apply maximum force to an object, maintain contact with the ground while the object is being accelerated.

Stretch Reaction: To develop maximum force, precede each muscular contraction with an initial stretch.

Absorption of Force: To absorb an impact, spread the force over the maximum area and the maximum distance possible.

Appendix C

Training Effects of Endurance Exercise upon the Cardiovascular System

Research during the last several years has clearly demonstrated that regular physical exercise of sufficient intensity and duration can produce remarkable adaptations in the cardiovascular system. Beneficial physiological changes take place in the heart, the blood vessels, the blood itself, and the musculo-skeletal system. There appears to be an all-or-none law that triggers these internal developments. The three components necessary for cardiovascular improvement are: 1) an exercise intensity sufficient to raise the heart rate to approximately 70 percent of maximum, 2) an exercise duration of at least 15 to 20 minutes and preferably longer, 3) an exercise frequency of at least three non-consecutive days per week and preferably more often. Although any physical activity that meets these criteria is acceptable, those which are rhythmical and easily controlled (e.g., walking, jogging, bicycling, stationary bicycling, swimming, rope jumping) seem most useful for promoting cardiovascular fitness.

What follows is a partial list of the training effects of an endurance exercise program. In addition to the incredible adaptations exhibited by the cardiovascular system, it is interesting to note that the untrained heart may contract about 40,000 more times per day than the trained heart in order to circulate the same blood volume.

Training Effects

I. Heart becomes a stronger pump.
    A. Stroke volume increases.
    B. Heart rate decreases.
        1. Heart has longer to rest.
        2. Heart has longer to fill with blood.
        3. Heart has longer to receive its own source of oxygen.
    C. Cardiac output increases.

II. Circulatory system becomes more efficient.
    A. Size of blood vessels increases.
    B. Number of blood vessels increases.
    C. Tone of blood vessels increases.
    D. Arterial blood pressure decreases.
    E. Efficiency of myocardial blood distribution increases.
    F. Efficiency of peripheral blood distribution increases.

III. Blood becomes a better transporter.
    A. Number of red blood cells increases.
    B. Mass of red blood cells increases.
    C. Amount of hemoglobin increases.
    D. Amount of plasma increases.
    E. Total blood volume increases (about one quart in average male).
    F. Platelet stickiness decreases.
    G. Levels of triglycerides and cholesterols decrease.
    H. Electron transport capacity increases.
    I. Arterial oxygen content increases.

IV. Other beneficial adaptations.
    A. Glucose intolerance decreases.
    B. Obesity/adiposity decreases.
    C. Thyroid function increases.
    D. Growth hormone production increases.

Source: Fox, Samuel M., Naughton, John P., and Gormon, Patrick A. Physical activity and cardiovascular health. *Modern Concepts of Cardiovascular Health* 41(April, 1972): 20.

  E. Vulnerability to dysrhythmias decreases.

  F. Maximal oxygen uptake increases.

  G. Endurance of respiratory muscles increases.

  H. Endurance of locomotor muscles increases.

V. Other possible adaptations.

  A. Improved sleep.

  B. Improved digestion.

  C. Improved elimination.

  D. Improved tolerance to stress.

  E. Improved self-confidence/esteem.

  F. Improved "joie de vivre" including mental and emotional health.

Appendix D

Strength Training Checklist

The following guidelines are basic to a safe, enjoyable, and effective program of strength development. Review your personal training approach in terms of this checklist.

1. Wear a minimum amount of clothing (i.e., tee-shirt, shorts).
2. Wear well-made, supportive athletic shoes.
3. Provide ample space to ensure freedom of movement while performing weightlifting exercises.
4. Engage in a few minutes of warm-up activity (i.e., rope jumping) before beginning the weight workout.
5. Perform static stretching exercises appropriate for each of the muscle groups that will be stressed during the training session.
6. Lift and lower the weights with a moderate and controlled rhythm.
7. Keep the weights evenly balanced throughout the lifting movements.
8. Inhale and exhale with each repetition. Do not hold your breath when lifting weights.

9. Postpone your scheduled workout if the muscles are still fatigued and recuperating from the previous training session.

10. Attempt to maintain regular training days, but do not train when you are not feeling well (e.g., chest cold).

11. Maintain a weight training notebook for reference and motivational purposes.

12. Whenever possible, train with a partner for safety and encouragement.

13. Try not to compare yourself with others. Remember that each person develops muscular strength at a different rate due to inherent physiological and biomechanical factors.

14. Incorporate jogging, swimming, cycling, or some other endurance type activity into your overall training program. Such activities strengthen the heart and improve the function of the circulatory system to help meet the demands of larger, more active muscles.

15. Performing a few minutes of easy, large muscle activity (i.e., walking, jogging, swimming) after a strenuous weight training workout aids recovery by removing lactic acid from the muscles.

16. For optimal training effects, eat a wide variety of nutritious foods (i.e., meats, fruits, vegetables, dairy products, whole grains and nuts) and obtain ample sleep (seven to nine hours nightly).

Glossary

Abduction: Sideward movement away from the midline of the body.

Activity Time: Time spent in actual training activity (i.e., performing exercises) as differentiated from time spent in a training facility.

Adduction: Sideward movements toward the midline of the body.

Adenosine Triphosphate (ATP): The chemical compound that, when split, produces the energy for muscular contraction.

Anaerobic Glycolysis: The principal energy source for vigorous activity lasting between 30 seconds and 3 minutes.

Antagonistic Muscle: The muscle that produces the opposite joint action to the prime mover muscle.

Atrophy: Decrease in the cross-sectional size of a muscle.

Berger Program: A system of strength training in which the exerciser performs three sets of six repetitions each. All three sets are done with the 6RM weightload.

Bodybuilders: Persons who use strength training as a means for achieving a better muscular appearance, especially with regard to muscle size, shape, definition, and proportion.

Bodyweight Exercises: Exercises in which one's bodyweight serves as the resistance. Bodyweight exercises can be augmented by attaching barbell plates to the waist.

Circuit Training: A training program in which one moves immediately from an exercise for one muscle group (e.g., shoulders) to an exercise for a different muscle group (e.g., abdominals), and so on until each major muscle group has been worked.

Concentric Contraction: A contraction in which a muscle exerts force, shortens, and overcomes a resistance.

Controlled Movement Speed: A weightload is raised and lowered in a slow and controlled manner to provide consistent application of force throughout the exercise movement.

DeLorme-Watkins Program: A system of strength training in which the exerciser performs three sets of ten repetitions each. The first set is done with 50 percent of the 10RM weightload, the second set is executed with 75 percent of the 10RM weightload, and the third set is completed with 100 percent of the 10RM weightload.

Direct Resistance: The resistive force is applied to the same body segment (e.g., upper arm) to which the movement force is applied.

Eccentric Contraction: A contraction in which a muscle exerts force, lengthens, and is overcome by a resistance.

Endurance: A measure of one's ability to continue exercising with a given, submaximum workload.

Extension: A movement that increases the joint angle between adjacent body parts.

Fasiculi: Groups of muscle fibers bound together by a membrane called perimysium.

Fast-Twitch Muscle Fibers: Muscle fibers that possess a greater capacity for anaerobic energy production.

First-Class Lever: Lever arrangement in which the axis of rotation is between the movement force and the resistance.

Flexion: A movement that decreases the joint angle between adjacent body parts.

Forced Repetition: A spotter can enable the exerciser to complete a lift that would otherwise be unsuccessful by giving a minimum amount of assistance. This procedure for more fully fatiguing the prime mover muscles is referred to as forced repetitions.

Free Weight: Barbells and dumbbells are usually referred to as free weights or loose weights because there are no restrictions on how they are utilized.

Full-Range Movement: Exercising a muscle through a complete range of joint motion, from a position of full extension to a position of full flexion, and vice versa.

Fusiform: Muscles characterized by relatively long fibers that run parallel to the line of pull.

High Intensity Training: Typically characterized by near-maximum weight-loads, as many repetitions per set as possible, and short recovery intervals between successive exercise bouts.

Hypertrophy: Increase in the cross-sectional size of a muscle.

Isokinetic Training: Training on apparatus that automatically varies the resistance in accordance with the applied muscle force. As muscle force increases the resistance increases proportionately, and as muscle force decreases the resistance decreases proportionately.

Isometric Contraction: A contraction in which a muscle exerts force, but does not change in length.

Lactic Acid: A fatigue producing by-product of anaerobic glycolysis.

Mini-Gym: One type of isokinetic training equipment that produces accommodating resistance by means of a hydraulic clutch and frictional forces.

Motor Unit: A single motor neuron and all the muscle fibers that receive stimulation from that nerve.

Muscle Balance: Maintaining a natural strength ratio between opposing muscle groups and training for overall muscular development, rather than specializing on particular muscles or exercises.

Muscle Belly: The actual muscle length between the tendon attachments.

Muscle Fibers: Groups of myofibrils bound together by a membrane called sarcolema, and innervated by a motor neuron.

Muscle Isolation: Designing training exercises so that the movement is accomplished to as large a degree as possible by a single muscle group, such as the Scott bench to focus on the biceps muscles.

Muscle Power: Technically, the rate at which work is performed. An increase in the speed of contraction, distance of contraction, or strength of contraction will produce a corresponding increase in muscle power.

Muscle Pump: Training that is characterized by many sets, many repetitions per set, and short rest periods between sets produces a greater saturation of the muscle tissue with blood that temporarily increases muscle cross-sectional area, and appears to be the most effective means for achieving muscle hypertrophy.

Myofibrils: The principal threads running throughout the muscles, myofibrils are formed from adjacent sarcomeres.

Nautilus Sports Equipment: Perhaps the most effective type of strength training equipment, many Nautilus machines provide direct resistance, rotary movement, and automatically variable resistance by means of an oval cam and chain arrangement.

Near-Maximum Resistance: Weightloads exceeding 75 percent of maximum are most effective for developing muscle strength, and are referred to as near-maximum resistance.

Olympic Lifters: Persons who train with weights in order to lift heavier weightloads in their competitive events, the clean and jerk and the snatch.

One Repetition Maximum (1RM): The heaviest weightload a person can lift once is called the one repetition maximum (1RM) weightload.

Paired Exercises: Following an exercise for a given muscle group with an exercise for the antagonistic muscle group. For example, performing leg curls (hamstrings) upon completing leg extensions (quadriceps).

Penniform: Muscles characterized by relatively short fibers that run diagonally to the line of pull.

Phosphagen: The primary source of energy for vigorous activity of a few seconds duration.

Powerlifters: Persons who train with weights in order to lift heavier weightloads in their competitive events, the squat, dead lift, and bench press.

Pre-Stretching: A quick stretching (lengthening) of a muscle just prior to contraction that enables the muscle to produce greater force.

Prime Mover Muscle: In any given joint action, the muscle that contracts concentrically to accomplish the movement.

Pyramid Program: A system of strength training in which the exerciser performs successive sets utilizing increasing weightloads and decreasing repetitions. The Westcott Pyramid Program consists of ten repetitions with 55 percent of the 1RM weightload, five repetitions with 75 percent of the 1RM weightload, and one repetition with 95 percent of the 1RM weightload.

Rebuilding Time: The time required for the muscles to rebuild to a higher level of strength following a training session.

Reciprocal Innervation: The nervous regulatory process that enables an antagonist muscle to relax and lengthen when a prime mover muscle contracts and shortens.

Recovery Time: The rest time allowed for the muscles to partially recover between successive sets of exercise.

Repetitions: The number of times an exercise is performed in succession. For example, the exerciser who takes the barbell from the floor, presses it ten times, and returns it to the floor has completed one set of ten repetitions.

Rotary Movement: Movement in a circular pathway, ideally with the resistance axis of rotation in line with the joint axis of rotation.

Sarcomere: The smallest functional unit of muscle contraction, a sarcomere consists of thin actin filaments, thick myosin filaments, and tiny cross-bridges which serve as coupling agents between these two protein structures.

Second-Class Lever: Lever arrangement in which the resistance is between the axis of rotation and the movement force.

Set: The number of separate exercise bouts performed. For example, the exerciser who does ten bench presses, rests a minute, then does ten more bench presses has completed two sets of ten repetitions each.

Six Repetition Maximum (6RM): The heaviest weightload an exerciser can lift six times in succession is referred to as the six repetition maximum (6RM) weightload.

Slow-Twitch Muscle Fibers: Muscle fibers that have a greater capacity for aerobic energy production.

Spotter: A training partner who gives assistance with an unsuccessful lifting attempt, adds resistance during an exercise, provides encouragement and feedback, and otherwise helps the exerciser train in a safe and effective manner. Spotters should be present in exercises such as the bench press and incline press for safety reasons.

Stabilizer Muscle: A muscle that stabilizes one joint so that the desired movement can be performed in another joint.

Strength: A measure of one's ability to exert muscular force against a resistance.

Strength Plateau: A period of time during which no further strength gains occur. It indicates that some aspect of the training program should be changed to enable further progress.

Strength Quotient: A means of comparing muscle strength among individuals of different sizes. The strength quotient is determined by dividing the maximum weight lifted in a given exercise by the exerciser's bodyweight. For example, a 150 pound person who can bench press a maximum weightload of 300 pounds has a strength quotient of 2.0.

Stress Adaptation: The ability of a muscle to respond positively to progressively greater training demands by gradually increasing contractile strength.

Stress Intensification: Progressively increasing the contractile demands of the muscles by training with more resistance, more repetitions, more sets, shorter rest intervals, or combinations of these factors.

Stretch Reflex: When a muscle is suddenly stretched, specialized control mechanisms called muscle spindles automatically trigger a rapid and forceful muscle contraction known as the stretch reflex or myotatic reflex.

Ten Repetition Maximum (10RM): The heaviest weightload an exerciser can lift ten times in succession is referred to as the ten repetition maximum (10RM) weightload. This generally can be accomplished with a 75 percent of maximum weightload.

Third-Class Lever: Lever arrangement in which the movement force is applied between the axis of rotation and the resistance.

Training Specificity: Training in a specific manner to achieve specific objectives. For example, leg extensions with a 10RM weightload would be more effective for strengthening the quadriceps muscles than a ten mile run.

Universal Gym: One type of isotonic exercise machine that provides a variety of exercise stations at which smooth running weight stacks are lifted by lever and pully attachments.

Valsalva Response: Holding the breath during a strenuous lifting movement produces increased pressure in the chest area, which can interfere with venous blood return to the heart and significantly elevate blood pressure.

Variable Resistance Training: Training on an apparatus that automatically changes the resistance throughout the exercise range of movement to accommodate the variations in muscle strength at different joint angles.

Work: The amount of work performed is the product of the force (weightload) multiplied by the distance travelled.

Bibliography

Astrand, Per-Olof and Rodahl, Kaare. 1970. *Textbook of work physiology.* New York: McGraw-Hill.

Berger, Richard A. 1962*a.* Comparison between resistance, load and strength improvement. *Research Quarterly* 33:637.

Berger, Richard A. 1962*b.* Effects of varied weight training programs on strength. *Research Quarterly* 33:168–181.

Berger, Richard A. 1962*c.* Optimum repetitions for the development of strength. *Research Quarterly* 33:334–338.

Berger, Richard A. 1963. Comparative effects of three weight training programs. *Research Quarterly* 34:396–397.

Berger, Richard A. 1965. Comparison of the effects of various weight training loads on strength. *Research Quarterly* 36:141–146.

Clarke, H. Harrison. 1971. *Physical and motor tests in the Medford boys' growth study.* Englewood Cliffs, New Jersey: Prentice-Hall.

Clarke, H. Harrison. 1973. Toward a better understanding of muscular strength. *Physical Fitness Research Digest* 3.

Clarke, H. Harrison. 1974. Development of muscular strength and endurance. *Physical Fitness Research Digest* 4.

Cooper, Kenneth H. 1968. *Aerobics.* New York: M. Evans.

Corbett, John J. 1969. The effect of different frequencies of weight training on muscular strength. Master's thesis, University of Western Ontario.

Corbin, Charles B. 1973. *A textbook of motor development.* Dubuque, Iowa: Wm. C. Brown.

Corbin, Charles B., Dowell, Linus J., Lindsey, Ruth, and Tolson, Homer. 1978. *Concepts in physical education.* Dubuque, Iowa: Wm. C. Brown.

Darden, Ellington. 1977. *Strength training principles: How to get the most out of your workouts.* Winter Park, Florida: Anna Publishing Co. Inc.

Dyson, Geoffrey. 1977. *The mechanics of athletics.* New York: Holmes and Meier.

Edelstein, Elliott Sheldon. 1964. Changes in strength, girth, and adipose tissue of the upper arm resulting from daily and alternate day progressive weight training. Master's thesis, Temple University.

DeLorme, Thomas L., and Watkins, Arthur L. 1978. Techniques of progressive resistance exercise. *Archives of Physical Medicine* 29:263.

Falls, Harold B., Baylor, Ann M., and Dishman, Rod K. 1980. *Essentials of fitness.* Philadelphia: Saunders College/Holt, Rinehart and Winston.

Fox, Edward L. 1979. *Sports physiology.* Philadelphia: W. B. Saunders.

Getchell, Bud. 1979. *Physical fitness: a way of life.* New York: John Wiley and Sons.

Gordon, H. H. 1967. Anatomical and biomechanical adaptations of muscles to different exercises. *Journal of the American Medical Association* 201:755–758.

Hafen, Brent Q. 1981. *Nutrition, food, and weight control.* Boston: Allyn and Bacon.

Hatfield, Frederick C., and Krotee, March L. 1978. *Personalized weight training for fitness and athletics: from theory to practice.* Dubuque, Iowa: Kendall-Hunt Publishing Co. Inc.

Hettinger, Theodore. 1961. *Physiology of strength.* Springfield, Illinois: Charles C Thomas.

Hookes, Gene. 1974. *Weight training in athletics and physical education.* Englewood Cliffs, New Jersey: Prentice-Hall.

Ikai, M., and Steinhaus, A. H. 1961. Some factors modifying the expression of human strength. *Journal of Applied Physiology* 16:157–163.

Jones, Arthur. 1977. Specificity in strength training: the facts and the fables. *Athletic Journal* 57:70.

Kalas, John P. 1977. Fast-twitch, slow-twitch muscle fibers: what is the truth? *Athletic Journal* 57:26–28.

Karpovich, Peter V., and Sinning, Wayne E. 1971. *Physiology of muscular activity.* Philadelphia: W. B. Saunders.

Katch, Frank L., and McArdle, William D. 1977. *Nutrition, weight control, and exercise.* Boston: Houghton-Mifflin.

Kurtz, John Raymond. 1968. Comparison of three weight training programs upon the development of muscular strength. Master's thesis, Illinois State University.

Lamb, David R. 1978. *Physiology of exercise: responses and adaptations.* New York: Macmillan.

Mathews, Donald K., and Fox, Edward L. 1976. *The physiological basis of physical education and athletics.* Philadelphia: W. B. Saunders.

Myers, Clayton R. 1975. *The official YMCA physical fitness handbook.* New York: Popular Library.

O'Shea, Patrick. 1966. Effects of selected weight training programs on the development of muscle hypertrophy. *Research Quarterly* 37:95.

O'Shea, Patrick. 1969. *Scientific principles and methods in strength fitness.* Reading, Massachusetts: Addison-Wesley.

Parker, Robert B., and Marsh, John R. 1974. *Sports illustrated training with weights.* Philadelphia: J. B. Lippincott.

Pipes, Thomas V. 1979. High intensity, not high speed. *Athletic Journal* 59:60–62.

Pollock, Michael L., Wilmore, Jack H., and Fox, Samuel M. III. 1978. *Health and fitness through physical activity.* New York: John Wiley and Sons.

Rasch, Philip J. 1979. *Weight training.* Dubuque, Iowa: Wm. C. Brown.

Rasch, Philip J., and Burke, Roger K. 1978. *Kinesiology and applied anatomy.* Philadelphia: Lee and Febiger.

Redding, Norman L., Jr. 1971. Effects of two different weight training programs on strength increment. Master's thesis, University of Florida.

Riley, Daniel P. 1977. *Strength training by the experts.* West Point, New York: Leisure Press.

Sharkey, Brian J. 1975. *Physiology and physical activity.* New York: Harper and Row.

Stone, William J., and Kroll, William A. 1978. *Sports conditioning and weight training.* Boston: Allyn and Bacon.

Vigars, Robert. 1978. Strength development reviewed. *Track and Field Quarterly Review* 78:50–52.

Westcott, Wayne L. 1974. Effects of varied frequencies of weight training on the development of strength. Master's thesis, The Pennsylvania State University.

Westcott, Wayne L. 1976. Unpublished Research Study.

Westcott, Wayne L. 1978a. Maintaining pre-season conditioning throughout the season. *The Coaching Clinic* 16:31–32.

Westcott, Wayne L. 1978b. Physical fitness: what is it and why should it be included in secondary school programs? *National Association of Secondary School Principals Bulletin* 62:15–19.

Westcott, Wayne L. 1979a. Female response to weight training. *Journal of Physical Education* 77:31–33.

Westcott, Wayne L. 1979b. Maximizing muscular power. Paper read at Eastern Connecticut State College Sports Clinic, March 1979.

Westcott, Wayne L. 1979*c*. Strength training for distance runners. *Track and Field Quarterly Review* 79:61.

Westcott, Wayne L. 1979*d*. Weight training: a daily activity. *Journal of Physical Education* 76:58.

Westcott, Wayne L. 1979*e*. Weight training and muscle balance. Paper presented at Eastern Connecticut State College Sports Medicine Symposium, March 1979.

Withers, R. T. 1970. Effects of varied weight training loads on the strength of university freshmen. *Research Quarterly* 41:110–114.

Wright, James E. 1980. The physiology of fatigue and recovery. *Muscle and Fitness* 41:64, 121–122.

Zohman, Lenore R. 1974. *Exercise your way to fitness and heart health.* Englewood Cliffs, New Jersey: CPC International.

Index